IT TAKES ALL TYPES

It Takes All Types

✠ ✠ ✠

The guide for finding a job, changing careers, and understanding yourself at work

✠ ✠ ✠

John J. Arnopp

ISBN: 1-4107-6021-9 (e-book)
ISBN: 1-4107-6022-7 (Paperback)

Library of Congress Control Number: 2003095204

This book is printed on acid free paper.

Printed in the United States of America
Bloomington, IN

1stBooks – rev. 07/16/03

To my family, for putting up with me, my personality, and my career path. Thank you.

FORWARD

As I WRITE THIS, I look back on a career which at first glance appears to follow a meandering path. That's because my career has lacked a plan. I never visualized a long-term goal for my career, even though in each job I held I had short to medium range goals. The common thread running through all my jobs was that I followed my interests. This "jack of all trades" approach has worked for my personality, allowing me to explore a large number of interests and jobs, all, though, being rather analytical positions.

I am not advocating the meandering approach to everyone, and wouldn't even suggest it to all people of my personality type. But it does illustrate the point that choosing a career is not a one-time task filled with fear of making the wrong decision. No career path you choose will necessarily be permanent or irreversible. If a job or line of work looks interesting to you, then investigate it – get more information any way you can. It may not be something you will ever try, but knowing you have explored the possibilities will provide you with peace of mind, so that you will be less likely to regret your ultimate path later.

It Takes All Types

Knowing my personality and the personalities of the people around me has been invaluable at work (and in life). As human beings, the people one interacts with socially and at work all have their own types and differences, and knowing some of the inherent personality reasons for these differences will allow you to understand why many things are the way they are.

I was first exposed to Myers-Briggs in high school, and was fascinated by how accurate it was. But the only information available commonly to me was David Keirsey's *Please Understand Me*, which I read and reread and discussed with friends and family, who all felt that the type and temperament descriptions were uncanny. But still, there was no practical "now what?" advice for how to use the information. Understanding is powerful, but most people also want some advice to take action.

It is my hope that you will find that advice here, in a very practical way. Not only are there lists of jobs that are suited to your temperament and personality role, but that is coupled with information on the current salaries and availability. Realistically, we cannot all be in the one perfect job for us. But there is no reason why each of us cannot be in a job that is a good fit for us and which can pay us what we need for our desired lifestyle and level of education.

FOREWARD

The biggest thing to keep in mind as you read through the book and the lists of positions is not how to limit your search to jobs that will fit you, but rather to notice how many and varied the lists are. And these are simply a starting point.

Remember – you can do anything...

CONTENTS

CONTENTS

CHAPTER 1

YOU CAN DO ANYTHING

YOU CAN do anything. That is the message you were likely given as a child by your parents and teachers. And it's absolutely true. But this book is not about what you *can* do; it's about what you can do *well* and how to choose what you *will* do based on your innate personality. There are four basic types of people, and what type you are will make all the difference to you in approaching your work life, where you will spend over 25% of your time during your working years. Having a job or career that works with your specific personality is critical to both your success, and the success of the tasks you perform. Your personality – specifically, what is referred to as *temperament* and that is innate to you – and how it relates to your career is the subject of this book.

It Takes All Types

The general definition of innate is "inborn," implying a trait that is an absolute part of you. In evolutionary psychology, innate is used to refer to "the ease with which certain things but not others are learned."[1] Your temperament may or may not be hard-wired, that is to say under strict genetic control, but what is near certain is that your temperament is *congenital*, or "present at birth." Most parents of more than one child will be quick to confirm not only how different their children are, but also how young their children were when they noticed these differences. Their children had different and identifiable temperaments from an early age.

Just as children have identifiable personality differences from an early age, they also have different ways of operating and communicating with their parents and peers. These different behaviors can show up simply as quirks in the way they act, or as real strengths and weaknesses in their development. For example, some children, even from the time they are newborns, seem more active, while others are calmer. Some kids get a big smile on their face when they meet new people and start conversations right away, while others avert their eyes and hide behind their parents' legs.

These tendencies, identified so early on, become more apparent, if also more integrated, to the child's observers. My daughter, even before the age of one year, would get a great big sad face and begin to cry if she heard another child crying in public, such as in the supermarket. My wife and I would have to look through the aisles to find the crying child and show our daughter that he or she was really all right. On the other hand, when my son

---

[1] According to behavioral geneticist Robert Plomin.

2

was confronted with a crying or hurt child, he would be just as likely to laugh uncomfortably as to completely ignore the incident, if possible. These differences in their personality traits – apparent so early on – will serve them uniquely throughout their lives.

These traits generally do not diminish with time, but become stronger. That is because people learn to build upon what works for them. While we may have the ability to perform away from our natural style, we tend to prefer certain patterns of things that seem more natural to us. The child that does not like to make quick decisions generally does not become an adult capable of snap judgments, but rather becomes very good at careful deliberation before a conclusion. Not only does this feel more natural to them, but it serves them well; they are more likely to make the correct decision than if they forced themselves or were forced to act away from their natural preference.

Similarly, someone whose preference is for a harmonious and people centered workplace is not going to be happy in a situation where orders are handed down from on high without consideration of the personnel that must follow those orders. They need to know there has been consensus in the decision process and agreement on the direction that they will take. They want to feel that the needs of all employees have been considered.

Linking Your Career With Your Personality

If you look around at the most successful people in our society – today and in the past – at the most admired performers, politicians, scientists, and business leaders, you will find people who not only have an understanding of who they are, but also how to express that understanding of themselves. By and large, the most successful people in any endeavor are successful because they are using their strengths. These are to a large degree their inherent traits, which they recognize, cultivate, and express. For example, Microsoft's Bill Gates was driven to be where he is today. How much of his success resulted from being in the right place at the right time, we will never know. But what we do know is that the traits he possesses drive him to continue or he would have quit long ago to do what he really wanted, having made all his money. Well, Bill Gates must still be doing what he really wants, which is overseeing the company he founded. To be successful, you must have the alignment of inherent ability and increasing practice through use of that ability. Success will be the ultimate self-expression of who you are.

So what are these innate abilities and preferences people have, and how can you discover and use your innate abilities and preferences to help you find a rewarding career? This is where the study of temperament comes in. In this book, we will first take a look at what and where the jobs are (chapter 2). Chapter 3 covers the development of temperament theory, especially modern temperament theory, and examines the link to behavioral genetics. We then examine the four temperaments – Guardian, Artisan, Idealist, and Rational – and why certain career paths and job choices play to their strengths (chapters 4-11). Chapter 12 offers suggestions for getting the most out of your career path and approaches to take in your job search.

Use this book to look at your career choices based on the natural abilities and intelligence (primarily one of four "intelligences") you possess. Add to this your values and interests, and you will see traits that really pinpoint who you are, and result in a whole picture of you, rather than only focusing on your skills (what you "can" do) or simply on what interests you (what you "want" to do). The approach I take is to combine your skills, interests, and values with job functions that require those talents you possess, based on your temperament. Rather than being one-sided – asking either for the skills or the interests that fit the job requirements or your own requirements – you can have it all. The ideal career is one that plays to your personality and allows you to enjoy and develop your natural talents.

Someone who thrives on human interaction and helping others, and who also happens to be a talented sculptor, might find the lonely life of an artist draining. But put them in a job helping others, leaving pottery as an occasional hobby, and they can both thrive in people-oriented service and have an expressive creative outlet. Similarly, if you are someone who bases your self-worth on the respect of society, pushing yourself into a telephone marketing position, even if you were a good spokesperson for products you believed in, would not be the career for you if you thought that the company or you personally were not respected in the community because the sales tactics employed caused people to have a negative opinion of you and your firm.

It Takes All Types

Much of what is presented here will probably be a new way of looking at your career path and the career paths of others. This can help you not only with your job, but in understanding why the people and institutions around us function the way they do. For example, many people believe the media has a "liberal" bias. If you look at the temperament of people who like to write and sometimes crusade for truth, traits commonly seen in journalists and reporters, you will invariably find "Idealists." Idealists are the antithesis of those types who value the stability of society and the *status quo* (called "Guardians"). Therefore, it comes as no surprise that those who would keep things as they are for the sake of stability and order would consider the media "biased." However the bias may really lie in the preferences of our personality.

On the other hand, people who don't stand on ceremony or tradition, who see things either as they should be in some idealized world ("Rationals") or as a means to an end in a purely practical way ("Artisans"), may have a very hard time with the rigid and bureaucratic rules of large organizations such as the U.S. Post Office (though neither of the former types would be ready to step into a career there). Meanwhile the temperament of the postal worker is one of stability, rules, order, and absolute impartiality with respect to being treated fairly and routinely in carrying out their tasks. It would work no other way.

As you read through this book, you should be able to identify your temperament with a little bit of reflection, or with the help of the "keyword indicator" in Chapter 3. This brief indication is not at all intended as a complete profiler, so if you are uncertain, or have difficulty, you can refer to the Resources section at the end and find places online to verify your temperament. With the knowledge of your temperament and the descriptions of the other temperaments, the world of organizations and individuals all doing things according to their natural preferences and personalities will begin to make more sense. You will start to see why various work systems function differently and often predictably. You will be able to choose the career setting that will fit you best, or be able to find the niche you need to be a success, however you ultimately define success for yourself. The truth is, depending on your temperament, you and the person sitting next to you at lunch may have very different ideas of a successful career.

CHAPTER 2

WHERE ARE THE JOBS?

So, WHERE ARE the jobs, and what are they? If you have looked at other career books, you will notice that there is a focus on professional and managerial occupations. While this excites people and sells an idealized view of your career, it leaves out the great majority of jobs that most people actually have. One of the key points of this book is a focus on the different types of people and how they can be most satisfied with their career or job, and not merely how a select group can get to the top of their profession. Sorry, not everyone who reads this book will end up as CEO of the next Microsoft. If you are looking mainly for tips on how to rise to the top of your profession, this book will help by helping you find your strengths and weaknesses. However, this book will be even more helpful to those of you looking at how to synthesize your career or job within the greater context of your life and personality. Also, if you are a career counselor or human resources manager, this book will help you to understand the people you interact with and what motivates them.

As mentioned above, managerial jobs are few and far between. In fact, they make up only 6% of all jobs, according to the National O*Net Consortium. The table below shows the percent of jobs in each major job category for the year 2000. While many people aspire to become management, few are really successful there, and even fewer happy in that role. Why is this? For starters, people desire managerial jobs for the prestige and compensation that accompany them. Others have a desire to influence and control. There is nothing inherently wrong with either of these motivations. However, of the two groups, the latter is much more likely to be successful as a manager than the former, because people who want to influence and control have associated behaviors that lead to greater success (like determination and risk-taking) versus the desire for a higher salary or a level of prestige, which are often associated with a desire for freedom and security.

Table of Occupations Categories, 2000

Occupational Category	Number of Jobs	Percent of Jobs
Office and Administrative Support	22,936,140	17.7%
Sales and Related	13,506,880	10.4%
Production	12,400,080	9.6%
Food Preparation and Serving Related	9,955,060	7.7%
Transportation and Material Moving	9,592,740	7.4%
Management	7,782,680	6.0%
Education, Training, and Library	7,450,860	5.7%
Construction and Extraction	6,187,360	4.8%
Healthcare Practitioners and Technical	6,041,210	4.7%
Installation, Maintenance, and Repair	5,318,490	4.1%
Business and Financial Operations	4,619,270	3.6%
Building and Grounds Cleaning and Maintenance	4,318,070	3.3%
Healthcare Support	3,039,430	2.3%
Protective Service	3,009,070	2.3%
Computer and Mathematical	2,932,810	2.3%
Personal Care and Service	2,700,510	2.1%
Architecture and Engineering	2,575620	2.0%
Arts, Design, Entertainment, Sports, and Media	1,513,420	1.2%
Community and Social Service	1,469,000	1.1%
Life, Physical, and Social Science	1,038,670	0.8%
Legal	890,910	0.7%
Farming, Fishing, and Forestry	460,700	0.4%

Where Are The Jobs?

The fundamental flaw in our occupational system is that there is more perceived prestige in being a manager or a professional than there is in being an office worker, a retail salesperson, or a "production" worker (a category which encompasses everything from tire builders and machine operators to power plant and equipment operators and from upholsterers and furniture makers to assembly line workers). While there is definitely more compensation in certain occupations – deserved or not – the real prestige should come from matching an individual's talent to their job. Not only does this make for the happiest and most fulfilling careers, but it is also much more productive for employers, employees, and the economy, with less friction as people move between jobs and careers.

The jobs presented in chapters 5,7,9, and 11 are jobs from entry level to apprentice to expert, encompassing all levels of education and salary. This way, you will be able to gauge how much education you really want or need to pursue for your career, which may be very different from the total amount of education you want or eventually will get. For example, there are numerous people with law degrees that do not practice law, largely because they were drawn to the idea of a profession, but do not like the actual tasks required. And, there are many people in occupations that do not require, or even make use of, the specific degree they earned in college. Does this mean that they do not value their education or degree? Not at all – simply that the education system is pretty inefficient at the job of matching the needs of employers to the training and skills it provides.

It Takes All Types

The college system is still largely based on the nobleperson's liberal arts education. Additionally, the number of trade school and high school vocational programs that were present during previous generations has steadily declined. Estimates place this loss at 60% of the programs disappearing over the last 30 years. Building these programs back up should be a major focus of our educational system. If not, many people who otherwise could find both training and validation for the jobs they will inevitably hold will be presented with a single path they will either not choose or not succeed in following. Both the employee and the employer will continue to lose.

To arrive at the jobs for the different personality types, I devised several algorithms to match a person's temperament to various aspects of the job. To assure the widest possible list of jobs and job characteristics, I used the O*Net database, created by the O*Net Consortium, which is a quasi-governmental agency sponsored by the U.S. Department of Labor. To arrive as salary levels, I used data from the U.S. Bureau of Labor Statistics that links to O*Net database. In this way, there is a standard "language" of job terminology and titles, which you can transport to any school counseling office or career coach.

What are the characteristics listed in the O*Net database? There are several, but generally the key factors used were the skills, activities, interests, and values of each job. These have been compiled by the Department of Labor over many years. The O*Net database lists over 1100 job classifications for over 12,000 specific job titles, and there are several different skills, activities, interests, and values for each job. For example, the data table of activities contains over 100,000 entries for the various jobs. Each of these was filtered against both the theoretical and actual preferences of the temperaments and their career roles. The interests for the temperaments are based on widely used interest areas developed by John Holland: realistic, investigative, artistic, social, enterprising, and conventional. You will encounter these interest areas in most assessments of skills and interests.

There are hundreds of job titles and larger classifications listed for the temperaments in this book, and they represent about 30% of the total employment of the United States. That means that even with these explorations of what should be the top career choices for each temperament, this is only the top of a pyramid of jobs that you can and should research in more depth. These jobs also span a wide range of skill levels and educational levels necessary for them. So you can narrow down the lists further by focusing on the level you are at, or on track to achieve. Even so, you might find a better fit at a different level than the one you are currently at, and will have to consider your lifestyle and relative satisfaction in choosing a job or career versus getting the training or education you need to pursue a job with a better fit.

I want to stress at this point that personality type and other job interest indicators, while very useful, cannot define the total measure of a person, even within a specific job role. Therefore, it is vital to your career success and happiness that you explore as many different job titles and functions as you can. You may already be very drawn to a particular career, or you may have no idea what could possibly interest you for a lifetime of work. Either way, please know that you have many options, and that if the point comes where you are not satisfied, there are many resources available to you.

Thus, you should be able to find a career that fits you or simply a job you can live with, on your way to the next thing. In addition to the skills you need, the activities you will perform, the interests you have, and the values you hold, please also keep in mind the environment you will be working within. This is as crucial as the other factors, but unfortunately not something that can be addressed here, since each workplace is different.

As a fun example of environment, consider the following four real companies, which have the names of the temperaments you will learn about in the next chapter: Guardian Life Insurance, Artisan Entertainment, Rational Software, and Idealist.org. Aside from being representative of why Dr. Keirsey chose the names he did for the temperaments, they also illustrate the different personalities companies can have. Guardian, true to its name, issues life insurance. Artisan Entertainment is in the business of producing and distributing movies. Rational Software is a computer software development company. And Idealist.org is a non-profit site that links volunteers with causes around the world. Not only do these companies have revealing names given them as part of the vision of their founders, the companies also have very different corporate structures and cultures.

CHAPTER 3

TEMPERAMENT THEORY

MODERN TEMPERAMENT THEORY is an extremely useful tool, but how did we get this tool? This chapter will give you an overview of where we've been, and then focus on where we are today.

THE PATTERN OF TEMPERAMENT IN HISTORY

Where we are today was largely developed by Dr. David Keirsey and popularized in his books *Please Understand Me* (1978) and *Please Understand Me II* (1998). But the theory and history of temperament goes back a long time, starting with Hippocrates, generally acknowledged as the father of Western medicine, in 400

It Takes All Types

B.C. Hippocrates related temperament to the four *humors* (bodily fluids) found in his patients, and called them *sanguine, phlegmatic, melancholic,* and *choleric.* This line of thinking about four basic types of people has been observed and intuited by many scholars and authors, and can be seen in the work and writings of Plato, Aristotle, Paracelsus, Jane Austen, Leo Tolstoy, D. H. Lawrence, Eric Adickes, Eduard Spränger, Ernst Kretschmer, Eric Fromm, William Sheldon, Isabel Myers, and David Keirsey.

The school of thought most associated with personality typing follows from Carl Jung, including Myers and Briggs. However, the model presented in Jung's *Psychological Types* (1923) was based on cognitive *functions* rather than temperaments. Jung proposed that people's motivation first could be thought of in terms of two basic attitudes, which Jung labeled *extraversion* (outward into the world of other people and objects) and *introversion* (inward into the realm of images, ideas, and the unconscious). The psychological functions that Jung saw underlying the extraversion and introversion orientation were *thinking, feeling, sensation,* and *intuition.* Thinking and feeling are decision-making functions, while sensation and intuition are information-gathering functions. It is from these combinations of functions and attitudes that we get the alphabet soup of E, I, N, S, T, F, J and P.

The Jungian/Myersian personality theory and its application can become quite complex as it attempts to explain the various aspects of the 16 personality types predicted. What is important is that the 16 personality types can be grouped into four temperaments, each with four sub-temperaments, or types. While this is not the way the pure Myers theory is used, many real-world practitioners have adopted the temperament approach to some degree. In fact, the descriptions of the 16 personality types written by most any practitioner of the Jung/Myers theory and the descriptions of the temperaments and their *role variants* (the sub-temperaments) are similar to, or even indistinguishable from, one another. Only the jargon used and the focus on the cognitive aspects of the Myers theory in contrast to the largely behavioral and observational aspects of temperament theory are different.

One of the modern temperament theorists who has contributed the most in terms of bringing the theory to people in a useful and approachable way is Dr. David Keirsey. In 1978, he published *Please Understand Me*, which popularized his work and study of temperament. In it, Keirsey outlined his theory, presented descriptions of the four temperaments and their role variants (also called personality types, of which there are 16 total), and included the first version of the *Keirsey Temperament Sorter*™ – a questionnaire designed to help you determine your temperament. The most current version of this questionnaire, along with other resources, is available on line at www.advisorteam.com.

⌘ ⌘ ⌘

It Takes All Types

Keirsey Temperament Theory and Intelligence Types

Abstract or Concrete?

At the heart of human nature, there exists one great difference between people. You have surely had conversations where you walk away saying "Where is that guy coming from?" or "She just doesn't get it." Maybe you've sat and listened to a guru or visionary, only to leave thinking nothing of substance was really said. Or you've read a plan or proposal that goes through painstaking sequential detail, but doesn't really address "the big picture" or capture your imagination. These are examples of the gap between types of people Keirsey calls *abstract* and *concrete*.

Abstract people, found in no more than 20% of the population, may be spotted by their spoken and written word usage. They tend to use analogies, fictional stories and examples, schematics, symbols, categories, and general principles. While we all spend time being both abstract and concrete, the abstract person spends the great majority of his or her time being introspective, as opposed to observant. The abstract, or introspective, person is often listening to an inner voice. The inner voice that speaks to the abstract person is, of course, based on observations, but not specific observations. Rather, it is based on patterns of observations and relationships between objects and people.

Abstract children can be identified as the ones that are always saying, "Oh, X is just like Y, with Z added; or so-and-so is related to my mom so that makes him related to me." They see patterns, categories, and relationships and want to understand how those relationships work at a "big picture" level. As adults, the tendency for abstraction generally becomes stronger, as years of practice harnessing this relationship-seeing ability is honed through use.

Concrete people make up the majority, greater than three-quarters, of society. Since most of the people you would tend to meet would be concrete, that is, exhibit a tendency toward observation, it might be hard to identify them other than as contrasted with the abstracters. All of us need to use our senses to take in information in all its forms: sound, sight, touch, taste, smell. Most of the time most of us are using our senses in this direct way, seeing what is there in front of and around us. But, as Keirsey points out, "Whatever isn't present to our senses we can only imagine by means of introspection."

Consider the well-worn analogy of the trees and the forest. While all of us, if dropped in the middle of a forest, would see trees, those that are more concrete would see and sense all the aspects of the trees. They would note the heights, colors, circumferences, number, density, and types of trees. They would notice the animal life and many of the forest's distinct smells. If asked, they would probably be able to tell you the path they took, the types of trees there, and the specific flavor profiles they smelled. By contrast, the more abstract person would envision the larger forest – that which could not be seen – and perhaps wonder how far it goes, what surrounds it, what habitats are present. Smells might trigger memories or associations (such as the time they went to get a Christmas tree as a child), and the light and shadow might put them into a certain mood. It is quite possible they would wander and become lost, or perhaps not remember their exact path. These are, of course, examples of the extremes, and both introspective and observant people will share both characteristics to a degree.

How do these distinctions look in practice, in the real world? The "dot-com" bubble at the end of the 20th century can be viewed in terms of the interplay between abstract and concrete people. In the early nineties, the concept of the World Wide Web took off, based on a network created largely for scientists and universities in the 1960's. This new instantaneous and ubiquitous communication method, with the ability to offer pictures and graphical links to pages related to each other, grabbed the imaginations of many people, largely people with observable abstract behavior. These were people such as Tim Berners-Lee, Marc Andreesson, Jim Clarke, Meg Whitman, Bill Gates, Kim Polese, and Steve Case. Literally thousands and thousands of business plans were written, for everything from web-based pet stores to online mortgages. Thousands of plans were funded and businesses started, from Netscape to Amazon.com and eBay to Webvan.

Still, with all this activity, there were many who were skeptical of the new gold rush. They did not invest in these businesses because they did not understand them, as these companies were not making money – previously a requirement for any investor. These were the "voice of reason" people, the sensible investors who watched as the rest of the world lost its head. These were the concrete investors who kept their money in traditional "brick-and-mortar" companies. The (largely abstract) business founders branded them as the ones who "Just don't get it."

At first, anyway. Then the concreters, being the observers of facts that they are, and being sensible people, took notice. They saw companies issuing stock to the public and watched as that stock's price doubled in one day. They saw money to be made and companies being built, seemingly overnight. They also saw new jobs being created, with inflated salaries. While many continued to remain skeptical, many also said, "This is the new economy, and it is working. If I invest, if I switch jobs and get stock options, I will make money too." And they did – for a while.

Of course, you know the outcome. The bubble eventually burst because in the end, the concreters were right in being doubtful of the prospects for many of the companies. So how did they get dragged into it in the first place? They watched what was working, and were not foolish to participate. The abstractors, for their part, lost more than money. They lost faith in their idealistic visions and grand conceptions, largely funded by money from concrete institutions like venture capital firms, banks, and wealthy friends and family. But, it was not a total bust. Some estimates say that in the last five years of the 20th century, more infrastructure and growth occurred in the Internet/technology arena than would have been possible at a more traditional, modest, and sustainable pace in 30 years. A look around shows how much has changed in people's life and the language they use to describe it in the last ten years. It also shows how much has not changed.

It Takes All Types

The Four Temperaments

When Keirsey first came across the work of Isabel Myers and the description she had written for his personality type, he knew that she was on to something. In examining the profiles and putting them together with his observations of people's behavior, he noted that the abstracters sort into two distinct groups, the *Idealists* and the *Rationals*, based on whether they are "tough-minded" or "tender-minded." Myers, following Jung, referred to these types as "thinking" and "feeling." In reality, we are all both thinking and feeling, though the way we primarily come to conclusions may be based more on either cooperative or utilitarian considerations. Thus, Keirsey sorts those who are *abstract* and *cooperative* (Myers' NFs) into the *Idealist* temperament and those who are *abstract* and *utilitarian* (Myers' NTs) into the *Rational* temperament. Each of these temperaments has four role variants. The table below shows the temperaments broken down into their role variants, and the Myers terminology for each, as well.

Tables of Temperaments and Their Role Variants

Temperament	Role	Role Variant	Myers' Label
Idealist	Mentor	Teacher	ENFJ
		Counselor	INFJ
	Advocate	Champion	ENFP
		Healer	INFP
Rational	Coordinator	Fieldmarshal	ENTJ
		Mastermind	INTJ
	Engineer	Inventor	ENTP
		Architect	INTP
Artisan	Operator	Promoter	ESTP
		Crafter	ISTP
	Entertainer	Performer	ESFP
		Composer	ISFP
Guardian	Administrator	Supervisor	ESTJ
		Inspector	ISTJ
	Conservator	Provider	ESFJ
		Protector	ISFJ

Similarly, Keirsey found that the concreters behaviorally fall into two main groups, the *Artisans* and the *Guardians*, based on whether they are "probers" or "schedulers." Myers referred to these types as "perceivers" and "judgers." While the terms are not symmetrical when viewed through the filter of Myers' theory, in Keirsey's temperament theory these two terms apply to either utilitarian or cooperative orientation, as with the abstracters. Thus, Keirsey sorts those who are *concrete* and *utilitarian* (Myers' SPs) into the *Artisan* temperament and those who are *concrete* and *cooperative* (Myers' SJs) into the *Guardian* temperament. Each of these temperaments also has four role variants, as shown in the preceding table.

The Intelligence Types

What David Keirsey has come to propose from his temperament theory is a theory of roles and intelligence types. Keirsey believes that intelligence is not represented merely, perhaps even at all, by measures of general cognitive ability – what we have all come to know as *intelligence quotient* or "IQ." Other proposed measures of "intelligence" may come closer to embodying the temperamental distinctions between people. For example, "emotional intelligence," popularized by Daniel Goleman but with roots in the early 20th century, or the "multiple intelligences" proposed by Howard Gardner. In essence, each person has four intelligences. But people of a particular temperament show one primary intelligence: Diplomatic, Strategic, Tactical, or Logistical. The other three trail the primary intelligence, to varying degrees.

Guardians, the concrete cooperators, possess the *Logistical Intellect*. Logistics is defined as the methods of procuring, maintaining, and replacing supplies and personnel, and this characterizes the Guardians, with their primary orientation towards the right people at the right place at the right time with the right resources. They work with the tools at hand in the prescribed manner to finish the job. Guardians are natural administrators, conservators, inspectors, supervisors, providers, and protectors.

They keep all the functions of a well-ordered society humming along. Keirsey presents George Washington, in his ability to keep his troops equipped and protected and also as the first president of the United States, as a prime example of the Guardian.

Artisans, the concrete utilitarians, possess the *Tactical Intellect.* Tactics, the art of attaining a military goal or other objective, is characterized by execution in the present – the immediate moment. Tactics are not only implied in battle or competition, but more broadly in any endeavor that requires the immediate reading or sensing of data input. Artisans are natural trouble-shooters, promoters, crafters, performers and composers. They work within their immediate time and space to manipulate equipment and tools of all types, including themselves, to achieve the tactical advantage over the competition, the audience, or the medium (e.g., clay, paint and canvas, or mechanical parts). General George Patton, clearly a talented *tactical intellect,* is a prime example of the Artisan.

Idealists, the abstract cooperators, demonstrate the *Diplomatic Intellect.* This is characterized by a natural tact in dealing with other people, an ability to empathize and communicate on a deeply personal level, and a gift for creating harmony, unity, and inspiration in people and groups. Idealists are the natural mediators, counselors, advocates, and teachers in the broad sense of those terms. The Idealist sees relationships and patterns in people, and works to bring those into alignment according to the harmonious patterns inherent in the Idealist's vision of how things should be. The person Keirsey gives us as an example of the diplomatic intellect – the Idealist – is Gandhi.

Rationals, the abstract utilitarians, possess the *Strategic Intellect*. Characterized by seeing relationship and patterns in complex systems, the Rational seeks to increase efficiency in these systems. These systems can be biological, social, mechanical, or operational. Rationals are natural problem-solvers, coordinators, inventors, and architects. They work to bring the ideal of efficiency and perfection inherent in their vision of how things should be to the systems they work with. Albert Einstein is an example of the strategic intellect – the Rational – working to improve the theories of the way the universe, the ultimate system, works.

A Quick Keyword Temperament Indicator

You may have a pretty good idea of which temperament fits you best. If you do not, you probably will when you read the four temperament descriptions in chapters 4,6,8, and 10. Looking at the keywords often associated with each temperament may also assist you. Read through the keywords below for each temperament (some appear for more than one temperament) and decide which group fits your preferences most closely. Finally, you can turn to the Resources section at the end of the book if you are still undecided.

Keywords Associated With The Four Temperaments	
Artisans	**Guardians**
experiences, excitement, realistic, sensation, actual, down-to-earth, utility, facts, practical, sensible, pending, flexible, adaptable, open-ended, tentative, unplanned, bold, clever, optimistic, action	society, experiences, facts, realistic, perspiration, actual, factual, practical, sensible, settled, fixed, stable, secure, punctual, dependable, responsible, planned, thorough, decided, loyal
Idealists	**Rationals**
future, speculation, inspired, possible, fantasy, intuition, imagination, values, people, fairness, humanity, harmony, appreciation, sympathy, compassion, empathy, devotion, fairness, warmth	intuition, inspiration, potential, hunches, calm, pragmatic, ingenious, inventive, objective, truth, impersonal, principles, justice, firmness, timeless, control, analysis, science, fiction, abstraction

BEHAVIORAL GENETICS

Behavioral genetics is a specialty that seeks to apply the strategies of genetic research to the study of human behavior. Genetics, particularly with the recent effort of the Human Genome Project, is clearly a central force in the life sciences. Genetic research in temperament has blossomed in the last decade through the work of hundreds of scientists in many disciplines. There are both basic and applied research programs at many of the leading universities throughout the world. As this work progresses, psychology – which is the science of emotions, behavior, and the mind – will take its place as a biological science. Genetics, specifically behavioral genetics, will be responsible for the bridging of the current gap between psychology and biology.

Looking at the complex human psychological-biological system, we see that the four temperaments are not evenly distributed. Guardians comprise about 45% of the population, Artisans about 35%, Idealists about 12%, and Rationals about 8%. While the U.S. population may be different from the rest of the world, and each region may have different distributions, it easy to see that you would not want 50% or more "abstracters" (Idealists and Rationals). It would probably not be a stretch to say that the underpinnings of society – the real schedules, routines, repairs, and documentation that keep things humming – would break down and collapse. And on the other hand, having no abstracters might literally create a society without vision and planning, both for its systems and the people within them.

Behavioral genetics can also help explain the relative frequencies of the temperaments in the population, and why they are not simply four equal groups. Behaviors, like other traits, sort randomly and are acted upon by selection in the environment. Over many generations, the more successful traits should have higher frequencies *in those environments where the traits are more beneficial*. But there are cases where harmful traits persist because in another degree, there is some benefit.

Temperament Theory

The classic example of this is sickle cell anemia, where inheriting two genes, one from both parents, causes a painful and sometimes fatal disease. But inheriting only one gene is actually more beneficial than no sickle genes in environments where malaria is a problem – the same places where high levels of the sickle gene are present in the population. The reason these genes persist (even in populations where there is no malaria) is because the selecting factors have been removed. Even if having one – or two – sickle genes is not beneficial in an environment, with modern medicine the people with these genes can often live as ordinary a life as if they did not have any sickle genes.

Another example is the discovery of a gene for "sensation seeking." People with this gene have an identifiable set of traits, including risk-taking. Looking back at human evolution, we can see how it would be important for some people, but not all, to have such a gene. These people would be the ones likely to find food when food was scarce, perhaps by taking a risk to capture prey. They would also be those willing to explore unknown territory (like mountains, caves, and lakes), making sure they were safe and report back, if they were able. However, the risk-takers might also experience higher failure rates than others, leading to early deaths and limiting the successfulness of this strategy. But even so, the survival of those without this gene might depend on being around people who did have it. Now, however, there is much less selection acting for or against the sensation-seeking gene, and the amount of sensation-seekers in the population will change more slowly over time. Similarly the relative frequencies, or expression, of temperaments we see in the population may have been decided long ago when humans were fighting for survival in a very different environment. The frequencies we carry forward may largely reflect that environment.

This is a career manual. The main point in emphasizing the role of genetics in temperament is the same point in emphasizing the role of temperament in career selection: to help you gain an understanding of the underlying factors, causes, and mechanisms for why you are who you are and why you do what you do. It has helped many people focus on how they want to live, and the hope is that it will also help you.

CHAPTER 4

GUARDIANS

ROBERT IS A company man. He worked for the same firm for 29 years, rising from assistant controller to vice president of finance. After earning his college degree in accounting, Robert worked for the accounting firm Price Waterhouse for a few years until he was hired away by a client company where he then spent most of his career. He stayed through two ownership changes until the new owners eventually laid him off during an economic downturn. He then accepted a position with one of the former owners, where he handles all aspects of accounting and finance for a group of companies.

The aspects of Robert's career that he has enjoyed most revolve around integrating the smaller companies the business has acquired along the way. Robert worked closely with the smaller companies to bring them into the larger company's systems and procedures. Implementing new standards and systems was interesting and enjoyable for Robert, and looking at the tasks involved, would naturally appeal to his temperament. The things that have been most difficult for him are the "people things." When I asked him to explain, he said the dealings with people where they did not do what they said they would do. Specifically, business partners and associates that did not perform on time or in an acceptable manner, or staff that did not live up to their responsibilities, were disappointing to him. These failings are things a Guardian may accept, but can never understand.

Even though Robert's employers have quit on him in the past, he has never quit on them. In fact, one of the owners told me a story about Robert and when the company was going through a particularly tough stretch. He said that Robert had gone to him and said that he would stay until they were through the tough period, either way, but then he would have to find a new job in a more stable company. The owner (probably not a Guardian) chastised Robert for being somewhat of a fool, saying if he felt the company would not make it, he should leave now rather than risk being unemployed. Otherwise, if he did stay, the owner told him he would make it worth his while. Robert stayed and, as you know, became the top finance manager. It should not surprise you to learn that Robert is a Guardian.

People of the Guardian Temperament make up about 45% of the United States population. They are everywhere, and it's a good thing, too. Not only do Guardians like to view themselves as reliable, responsible, and dependable, but this is how others view them as well. If something needs to get done, the surest way to make sure that it will be done with no surprises is to put a Guardian in charge of it. I liken Guardians to a glue that holds society together; like the gravitational force that keeps everything from flying apart. Yes, at times glue is sticky. Gravity can be a drag, but consider the alternative.

Being almost half the population, it shouldn't be too hard to recognize your fellow Guardians. A look at their offices or workspaces should tell you that you are in the presence of a traditional and proper person. Things will not be out of order; in fact, they will likely be in a very specific order – alphabetical, chronological, by height, weight, or other standard classification scheme. Your Guardian coworkers are the ones that are always on time – even early – and who stick to the regular break and lunch schedules. Routine and order are synonymous with security and stability, which are two values that Guardians hold dear.

Some Guardians may seem very quiet and serious, while others appear more chatty or sociable, but all are likely to spend break times where people generally congregate. The exception will be when the Guardian does not take a break at all, bent on finishing a project on time or catching up on something they fear is falling behind. Guardians like to be where people are because it's people, in the form of groups, offices, affiliations, memberships, and clubs that attract them. Groups make up society, and society, when the people in it adhere to the rules and order, is stability and security.

It Takes All Types

Keirsey tells us that the Guardians are concrete in the use of words. You can use this to spot Guardians in conversation, where they will talk about details of everyday life, such as the weather, the commute, business, the day's news. This is often referred to as "small talk" but it's really not small. It is actually the world the Guardians, and other concreters, live in and allows them to function well in managing the details of their life and business in a way that minimizes disruption. If they did not keep tabs on the weather, the traffic, the stock market, or – for fun – the baseball season stats, they would not be able to carry out their logistical roles.

Guardians display the logistical intelligence. Logistics is the fundamental function of most business: ordering, storing, moving, distributing, and reordering products and hiring, firing, assigning, and managing personnel. This innate skill the Guardians display becomes more and more natural and ever more useful to them through practice. From an early age young Guardians will tend to collect and catalog things – coins, rocks, stamps, books, baseball cards – anything that can be collected and organized. Other temperaments will have collections, but none will be as orderly or complete as the Guardians. Even Rationals, who you might think would at least be the equal of the Guardians, will often lose interest before a collection is complete, or will arrange it once or twice according to their own scheme, and then abandon it to its natural random order.

Guardians are also cooperative in their tool use. In the broader sense of the word, almost everything physical around us is a tool:

our homes are tools for protection from the elements, cars are tools for moving ourselves, streets tools for carrying cars, and so on. All of these tools need rules and regulations to govern their use, for the safety of everyone. Homes must be built to code to prevent fires and other casualties; cars must be driven by licensed drivers who follow the rules of the road. Guardians conform to and obey the rules set up by society so that things do not degenerate into chaos. Stopping at the stop sign a block from home, even at 3 a.m. when no one else is on the road, makes the Guardian feel safe and secure, not impatient or silly.

As they enter the workforce, Guardians apply the skills they've deepened through years of developing their logistical intelligence to the problems of their business. The strategic goals of the Rational might be important, the Idealists' primary concern for the human factor is certainly recognized as important, but the tactics of the Artisan are to be avoided as dangerous, or at least unnecessary. Guardians are the reliable, organized, dependable, obedient, and accountable workers. They gravitate toward jobs where they can increase stability and security, which increases their sense of stability and security. When they accomplish these things, and are recognized for them, Guardians will increase their self-image.

THE SELF-IMAGE OF GUARDIANS

It is important to understand what makes up the self-image of others and ourselves if we are going to be able to effectively communicate, lead, follow, motivate, and appreciate each other in the workplace. Our self-image is composed of three main attributes: self-esteem, self-respect, and self-confidence.

The self-esteem of Guardians is tied to dependability, reliability, and accountability. When they see themselves and are seen by others this way, they can increase their self-esteem. Because of this, Guardians almost never say no to the addition of another task, working harder to be dependable, thus increasing their self-esteem. At the same time, they can worry they are not doing enough, become physically or mentally exhausted, and even ill and depressed.

Guardian self-respect comes from a sense that they are doing good for others and society. In particular, this good takes the same concrete form as the Guardian's own attitude toward good: security and stability. Thus, they will provide others with food, clothing, and shelter. This can take the form of donations of money to a homeless shelter, volunteering time at a Habitat for Humanity project, or transporting items to the old and infirm. Guardians can gain this self-respect in their careers, as well, often as teachers, public servants, medical occupations, or military personnel.

Self-confidence for Guardians arises from respectability. Guardians for the most part are modest and unassuming people who do not like to be seen or thought of as showy, flashy, or putting on airs of any kind. The respectability they seek needs to come not from any attention getting behavior they display, but from the consistent service they provide to their communities. Respectability for Guardians is shown by "official" recognition, such as diplomas, certificates, awards, honors, and other business or personal tokens. Of any of the temperaments, the engraved gold watch for a long and productive career is sure to be cherished and appreciated most by the Guardians.

ARCHETYPE AND CARICATURE

Keirsey presents George Washington as a prime example of the Guardian. He displayed the logistical intelligence of Guardians in abundance. Over eight years, Washington kept his outnumbered troops fed, clothed, sheltered, and out of danger long enough to achieve victory over the British. Washington was then called back into service as the first president of the new nation – a call to duty that he could not resist.

If George Washington is the archetype of a Guardian, then Major Frank Burns from the television series *M*A*S*H* is a perfect caricature. The series is set in a mobile army hospital during the Korean War. Major Burns is a caricature of the military, which is depicted as an institution based on rules, rank, bureaucracy, hypocrisy (for not all rules can live together harmoniously), war, and blind patriotism. Two of the doctors (Captains Hawkeye Pierce and B.J. Hunnicut) represent values of peace, life, human tolerance, and equality. They do not hold much respect for rules, regulations, or the army code of conduct, and are constantly targeted for disciplinary action by Major Burns, for even the minutest infraction.

Another example comes from the HBO series *Sex and the City*. The show revolves around the lives of four women living in New

York – each of whom seems to embody a different temperament. Charlotte, likely a Provider Guardian, is the most traditional of the four, which can be seen in the show's main theme and in her career. She worked as an art gallery director at a prestigious gallery serving New York's high society, but quit her job after getting married and trying to start a family. However, Charlotte and her wealthy doctor husband divorced, and she lives alone in her large flat, part of the divorce settlement. Still wanting to serve people and society in a respectable job, even though she was told she was "over-qualified" for any art gallery positions, she became a volunteer docent at the Metropolitan Museum of Art.

In one scene when the four women are talking about dating and the careers their boyfriends have, Charlotte says to Miranda, who is dating a bartender, "I don't know how you can get so serious with a guy who's entire future is based on tips." Charlotte, as a Guardian, views a stable, salaried job as necessary for a safe and secure future. And even when money is not an issue for stability, as in Charlotte's case, a respectable job, such as her volunteer work at the Met, is always a prime consideration.

MANAGING, LEADING, AND ENTREPRENEURSHIP

Guardians create stability in an organization – the policies, procedures and personnel used to create order. They enjoy and are good at making logical and practical decisions, which they will weigh and make based on the facts and common sense. If all the facts are not available, they will carefully set about getting the facts they need, not missing important details. Their colleagues usually know where the Guardian manager stands on an issue. They respect both that the manager will work hard for the organization and that he or she expects the subordinate to do the same. Coworkers usually see the Guardian manager as a taskmaster or as a loyal coworker, depending upon their own temperament.

As entrepreneurs, Guardians display these same positive traits. Because they are comfortable with order, they prefer to work with that which is known to them. They may become business managers by first having been a recognized manager of a group which has been spun off, leaving them in charge, or in a well-defined business model, such as a franchise. In either case, they will generally not lead autocratically, but will form a management team to lead the venture. Because of the need for stability – to have things settled – the Guardian leader may act too quickly in making decisions. This usually happens when business issues are unsettled, or in flux, where the Guardian lacks the adaptability to roll with the change and does not have the time to gather all the facts in an orderly way. However, in the standard state of an established business, a Guardian manager is an essential component to a winning team.

SKILLS, ACTIVITIES, INTERESTS, AND VALUES

In looking at career and job choices for the Guardians, we must consider the skills, activities, interests, and values of the person and the job. While your skills and interests may be different from other

Guardians, the jobs presented have been shown to be those that interest a large portion of Guardians and that display skills that build naturally on their logistical intelligence. There is a range of activities and skill levels in the jobs presented in the next chapter, and the list is by no means exhaustive. It is meant to both illustrate the principles of finding a job that fits your temperament well and to point you in a series of directions for the skill level you have acquired or are willing to acquire.

Guardians' skills are developed through use and practice of the logistical intellect. These skills, in the job language of the Occupational Information Network (O*Net) sponsored by the U.S. Department of Labor, are:

The Skills of Guardians

- Judgment and Decision Making
- Management of Financial Resources
- Coordination
- Implementation Planning
- Operation Monitoring
- Operation and Control
- Testing
- Information Organization
- Monitoring
- Equipment Selection
- Product Inspection
- Service Orientation
- Time Management

GUARDIANS

These are the skills that were primarily used in assessing the skill component of the Guardian jobs. It is not necessarily that all Guardians display great aptitude in all these skills, but only that you recognize the ability to attain these skills will come more naturally to you. The jobs and careers presented in the next chapter will require some or all of these skills, and you can enhance them by using your logistical intelligence.

There are 42 activities and over 100,000 activity entries for the 1100 jobs in the O*Net catalog. The top activities involved in the Guardian jobs are the following:

THE ACTIVITIES OF GUARDIANS
- Documenting/Recording Information
- Inspecting Equipment, Structures, Material
- Monitor Processes, Material, Surroundings
- Performing Administrative Activities
- Performing for/Working With Public
- Coordinating Work & Activities of Others
- Assisting and Caring for Others
- Monitoring and Controlling Resources
- Scheduling Work and Activities
- Organizing, Planning, and Prioritizing
- Updating & Using Job-Relevant Knowledge
- Staffing Organizational Units

These activities used in selecting jobs take full advantage of the Guardians' sense of duty, dependability, reliability, attention to detail, and service orientation.

The next factors that went into determining the top jobs for Guardians were their interests, based on six well-defined interest areas. They are:

- *Realistic* - Are you interested in jobs that require athletic or mechanical ability, working with objects, machines, tools, plants or animals, or being outdoors?
- *Investigative* - Are you interested in jobs with people who like to observe, learn, investigate, analyze, evaluate or solve problems?
- *Artistic* - Are you interested in jobs involving artistic, innovative or intuitive abilities, and like to work in unstructured creative situations?
- *Social* - Do you like to work with people to inform, help, train, enlighten, develop or cure or are you skilled with words?
- *Enterprising* - Are you interested in jobs where you work with people to influence, perform, persuade, or lead for organizational goals or economic gain?
- *Conventional* - Are you interested in jobs that involve working with data, clerical tasks, or numerical ability, carrying things out in detail or following instructions?

42

Both the top interest areas and the order of their importance were used to filter good job matches for the Guardians.

Finally, a list of values appealing to Guardians was used to make sure that the jobs would match not only skills, activities, and interests, but key values. In fact, often the first thing you notice about another person is an expression of their values. For example, the top Guardian values are:

THE VALUES OF GUARDIANS

- Social Status
- Responsibility
- Achievement
- Authority
- Recognition
- Security
- Compensation
- Company Policies and Practices

If you have taken the Keirsey Temperament Sorter, and if the skills, activities and values above appeal to your sense of a job, then you are probably on the right track reading about Guardians. You should continue on to the next chapter with descriptions of Guardian roles and actual jobs. If not, please explore the chapters on the other three temperaments to find your ideal career.

CHAPTER 5

THE GUARDIAN ROLES

ACCORDING TO temperament theory, Guardians tend toward one of two roles: Administrator or Conservator, which differ enough from each other that there is a separate list of jobs for each.

ADMINISTRATORS – THE SUPERVISOR AND THE INSPECTORS

Administrators are the "tough-minded" Guardians, as Keirsey defines them. They take on the roles of regulating: enforcing and certifying. They are *role directive*, which means that they are more apt to take charge and tell others what to do. They are the image you get of a manager when you picture corporate America. Administrators come in two role variants – Supervisors and Inspectors – both of which share the tough-minded, directive traits.

Myers referred to the Supervisor as the ESTJ and the Inspector as the ISTJ.

Supervisors tend to be more expressive, working with the people in an organization within the context of the procedures, rules and regulations. Inspectors are more reserved, working less with the people in an organization and more with the input and output of the organization, either in quality control or accounting functions. They assure that the product standards are being met and that the books are in order.

When not satisfied in their current career, or when looking for a new career, Administrators are concerned with their experience for a new position. They have a hard time switching careers when they feel they may lack the proper training or required skills. For example, the following are typical Administrator reactions to job changes:

> I am worried. I will be losing my job in January most likely and don't know what to do. I have a college degree in computer science but don't have any experience in the real world in programming. I have worked at a start up for one year doing SQA (software quality assurance). My confidence level in programming is really low because I guess I didn't learn everything I should have at school, like networking. I don't even think I like my field anyway.

✼   ✼   ✼

It Takes All Types

> I have 8 years of military experience and 3 years staffing and staffing management experience. What types of career can I switch to where I won't need the years of experience to get in?

Jobs for Administrators

The jobs listed on the next pages are top matches for Administrators, but by no means the only careers you should consider. Listed next to each standard job classification are the total number of people employed in that occupation in the United States and the salary ranges. The "starting" salary is the number that 90% of people in that job earn more than. The "high" salary is the number that 90% of people in that job earn less than. So 80% of the people in a job earn between the starting and high salary figures. The "median" is the number that half the people earn more than and half earn less than. These are national averages, and you could earn more or less.

The jobs in bold are the "best of the best" for your temperament and role. These are based on the degree to which the job fit your personality and also the number of available jobs, relative to the amount of people of your temperament in the population. For example, Radio Mechanic would be a good job for an Administrator, but with only about 7,000 positions available nationwide, it would not be as helpful to list it as a top job. However, it helps to list it because the skill might be similar to another job you are considering, or it may point you in a direction that you would otherwise have missed.

Finally, the jobs are in rough order from the lowest skill level *for the skills required of the job* to the highest level. For example, electric meter installer and repairer is the first job listed, and so would have a lower "level" than elevator installer and repairer. Both jobs would seem roughly equivalent, yet elevator installer/repairer has a higher level and is a top job (bold). This is because the top skills of the Administrator are more important to the elevator job (as defined in the O*Net database) than to the electric meter job.

Best Fit Jobs for Administrators (Supervisors and Inspectors)

Job Title	Estimated Employment	Salary		
		Starting	Median	High
Electric Meter Installers and Repairers.	34,910	23,470	41,330	57,180
Sound Engineering Technicians.	**10,380**	**17,560**	**39,480**	**119,400**
Gaugers.	31,230	28,220	45,180	57,040
First–Line Supervisors/Managers of Food Preparation and Serving Workers.	**624,180**	**14,870**	**22,680**	**37,740**
Rail–Track Laying and Maintenance Equipment Operators.	9,940	18,590	31,060	43,230
Gas Appliance Repairers.	33,910	17,300	28,860	45,750

Elevator Installers and Repairers.	25,100	23,280	47,380	69,120
Medical Records and Health Information Technicians.	143,870	15,710	22,750	35,170
Bus Drivers, Transit and Intercity.	175,470	15,890	25,710	41,660
Power Generating Plant Operators, Except Auxiliary Equipment Operators.	34,720	28,700	46,090	62,020
Electric Motor and Switch Assemblers and Repairers.	36,620	18,980	32,860	52,360
Electrical and Electronics Repairers, Powerhouse, Substation, and Relay.	19,300	30,760	48,540	60,320
Radio Mechanics.	7,110	19,540	32,990	53,290
Engine and Other Machine Assemblers.	66,090	16,800	28,010	44,680
Chemical Equipment Tenders.	60,380	23,060	35,800	51,660
First–Line Supervisors and Manager/ Supervisors– Construction Trades Workers.	502,010	28,660	44,790	70,780

First–Line Supervisors/Managers of Mechanics, Installers, and Repairers.	421,740	26,860	44,250	70,090
Maintenance Workers, Machinery.	107,500	19,150	30,970	47,310
Food Service Managers.	**282,290**	**19,200**	**31,720**	**53,090**
Semiconductor Processors.	**67,000**	**18,410**	**25,430**	**39,720**
Cooling and Freezing Equipment Operators and Tenders.	7,410	13,570	20,180	34,140
Claims Examiners, Property and Casualty Insurance.	189,700	25,860	41,080	68,130
Signal and Track Switch Repairers.	5,540	28,240	40,030	51,400
Financial Analysts.	159,490	31,880	52,420	101,760
Maintenance and Repair Workers, General.	1,216,250	16,320	27,850	44,570
Machinists.	420,320	18,740	30,740	45,430
Millwrights.	75,940	25,000	40,210	56,300
Municipal Fire Fighting and Prevention Supervisors.	59,500	31,820	51,990	77,700

Chemical Equipment Controllers and Operators.	**60,380**	**23,060**	**35,800**	**51,660**
Boilermakers.	25,280	19,980	37,020	55,770
Metal Molding, Coremaking, and Casting Machine Operators and Tenders.	158,280	14,650	21,620	35,220
Riggers.	14,640	18,820	32,080	48,900
Model Makers, Metal and Plastic.	10,540	15,570	33,420	61,420
Elementary School Teachers, Except Special Education.	1,409,140	25,810	39,700	62,600
Forest Fire Fighting and Prevention Supervisors	**59,500**	**31,820**	**51,990**	**77,700**
First–Line Supervisors, Customer Service.	**1,394,640**	**22,070**	**36,420**	**60,600**
Data Processing Equipment Repairers.	142,390	19,760	31,380	48,720
Police Patrol Officers.	571,210	23,790	39,790	58,900
Anesthesiologists.	24,350	88,170	*	*
Technical Directors/Managers.	**46,750**	**21,050**	**41,030**	**87,770**
Product Safety Engineers.	**42,800**	**34,710**	**54,630**	**82,320**
Air Traffic Controllers.	23,350	44,760	82,520	111,150

Biochemists.	13,440	32,310	54,230	93,330
Highway Patrol Pilots.	571,210	23,790	39,790	58,900
Station Installers and Repairers, Telephone.	192,470	25,050	44,030	56,630
Ship and Boat Captains.	**21,080**	**23,280**	**47,510**	**73,090**
Transportation Managers.	**116,680**	**31,470**	**54,230**	**90,730**
Program Directors.	**46,750**	**21,050**	**41,030**	**87,770**
Construction Managers.	**229,200**	**34,820**	**58,250**	**102,860**
Financial Managers, Branch or Department.	622,890	36,050	67,020	131,120
Fish and Game Wardens.	7,730	25,960	39,950	67,030
Industrial Production Managers.	**205,370**	**35,530**	**61,660**	**106,020**
Database Administrators.	108,000	29,400	51,990	89,320
Sales Agents, Securities and Commodities.	269,310	24,770	56,080	*
First–Line Supervisors/Managers of Police and Detectives.	113,740	34,660	57,210	86,060
Civil Engineers.	207,080	37,430	55,740	86,000
Airframe–and–Power– Plant Mechanics.	135,730	25,080	40,550	56,100
Pharmacists.	**212,660**	**51,570**	**70,950**	**89,010**

Economists.	13,680	35,690	64,830	114,580
Pile–Driver Operators.	4,320	22,850	41,290	64,560
Computer Systems Analysts.	463,300	37,460	59,330	89,040
Engineering Managers.	242,280	52,350	84,070	130,350
Aircraft Engine Specialists.	135,730	25,080	40,550	56,100
Education Administrators, Postsecondary.	**92,280**	**32,650**	**59,480**	**109,280**
Computer Programmers.	530,730	35,020	57,590	93,210
Computer Security Specialists.	234,040	32,450	51,280	81,150
Orthodontists.				*(no data available)*
Mechanical Engineers.	207,300	38,770	58,710	88,610
Airline Pilots, Copilots, and Flight Engineers.	**94,820**	**36,110**	**110,940**	*
Commercial Pilots.	**18,040**	**24,290**	**43,300**	**92,000**
Postmasters and Mail Superintendents.	**26,850**	**35,380**	**44,260**	**64,960**
Administrative Law Judges, Adjudicators, and Hearing Officers.	12,560	32,970	61,240	111,590

Arbitrators, Mediators, and Conciliators.	4,850	23,360	43,060	93,170
Government Service Executives.	519,890	46,390	113,810	*
Mining and Geological Engineers, Including Mining Safety Engineers.	6,690	36,070	60,820	100,050
Computer Software Engineers, Applications.	**374,640**	**42,710**	**67,670**	**106,680**
Computer Software Engineers, Systems Software.	**264,610**	**43,600**	**69,530**	**105,240**
Computer Hardware Engineers.	**63,680**	**42,620**	**67,300**	**107,360**
Podiatrists.	7,870	48,130	107,560	*
Criminal Investigators and Special Agents.	87,090	29,600	48,870	72,160
Psychiatrists.	21,280	50,930	118,640	*
Veterinarians.	40,270	36,670	60,910	128,720
Private Sector Executives.	519,890	46,390	113,810	*
Chemists.	82,320	29,620	50,080	88,030
Judges, Magistrate Judges, and Magistrates.	**25,190**	**19,320**	**86,760**	**134,660**

Technical Writers.	50,700	28,890	47,790	74,360
Treasurers, Controllers, and Chief Financial Officers.	622,890	36,050	67,020	131,120
Family and General Practitioners.	132,620	44,970	114,170	*
Internists, General.	50,450	77,720	142,400	*
Obstetricians and Gynecologists.	18,240	98,490	*	*
Pediatricians, General.	25,580	77,980	125,970	*
Chemistry Teachers, Postsecondary.	16,020	30,870	52,530	89,390
Biologists.			*(no data available)*
Geologists.	21,810	33,910	56,230	106,040
Statisticians.	17,520	28430	51990	86660
Lawyers.	**489,530**	**44,590**	**88,280**	*
Computer Science Teachers, Postsecondary.	27,770	24,980	46,890	85,490
Aerospace Engineers.	71,550	47,700	67,930	94,310
Chemical Engineers.	31,530	45,200	65,960	93,430

*Indicates a salary greater than $145,000 per year.

Bold indicates this is a top job, based on both fit and/or total employment.

The Guardian Roles

The jobs listed here are just the beginning. It is important to read through all the jobs for your temperament, and to browse the jobs for the other temperaments. This will ensure that you have identified your temperament correctly. Then, refer to chapter 12 for where to go from here.

Conservators – the Providers and the Protectors

Conservators are the "friendly" Guardians, according to Keirsey. They take on the roles of supporting; supplying and securing. They are *role informative*, which means that they are more apt to keep records, write reports, and give accounts than to give direct orders. Conservators come in two role variants – Providers and Protectors – both of whom share these friendly, informative traits. Myers referred to the Provider as the ESFJ and the Protector as the ISFJ.

Providers tend to be more expressive, working to provide people in an organization or society with whatever they need for their general welfare, through jobs such as banker, distributor, sponsor, and supplier. Protectors are more reserved, working less with the people they serve in an organization and more behind the scenes, often as a caretaker, insurer, preservationist, public safety officer, or treasurer. They support the institutions they serve by being responsible for the supplies and people within their care.

When not satisfied in their current career, or when looking for a new career, Conservators, like the Administrators, focus on getting the training and education they need. They seek on-the-job training and programs that are specific to their needs. For example, the following are typical Conservator reactions to job changes:

> I am preparing to make a third life-change. I started out as a Registered Nurse but heeded my longings and went back to school, getting first a Masters, then a PhD, in English literature. I am a specialist in renaissance and medieval English but have basically spent the last 12 years learning to research and write. I also have taught others to write. I am helping provide care for aging and frail parents – moving is out of the question. I also teach part time at a local college, but the pay is not great. I am a warm, caring person and an excellent teacher. I worked retail during grad school and ended up doing corporate training. I would like to use my research and writing skills but haven't a clue how to get started.

❊ ❊ ❊

> I'm 46 years old and have done mostly temp work while I was raising my family. Through my temp work and love of computers I have developed good administrative assistant skills. I'm a fast learner and self-teacher when necessary. I love to write and have been told by several people that I should be a writer. My brother, sister and I were talking about my characteristics, likes, etc. and we came up with paralegal (because I love investigating things, figuring things out, and writing) and a school counselor or something like that. Is it too late for

me to go to school and actually find work in these areas? What kind of work could I do in the meantime to help find a job in future?

JOBS FOR CONSERVATORS

The jobs listed on the next pages are top matches for Conservators, but by no means the only careers you should consider. Listed next to each standard job classification are the total number of people employed in that occupation in the United States and the salary ranges. The "starting" salary is the number that 90% of people in that job earn more than. The "high" salary is the number that 90% of people in that job earn less than. So 80% of the people in a job earn between the starting and high salary figures. The "median" is the number that half the people earn more than and half earn less than. These are national averages, and you could earn more or less.

The jobs in bold are the "best of the best" for your temperament and role. These are based on the degree to which the job fit your personality and also the number of available jobs, relative to the amount of people of your temperament in the population. For example, Fish and game Warden would be a good job for a Conservator, but with only about 7,700 positions available nationwide, it would not be as helpful to list it as a top job. However, it helps to list it because the skill might be similar to another job you are considering, or it may point you in a direction that you would otherwise have missed.

Finally, the jobs are in rough order from the lowest skill level *for the skills required of the job* to the highest level. For example, electric meter installer and repairer is the first job listed, and so would have a lower "level" than elevator installer and repairer. Both jobs would seem roughly equivalent, yet elevator installer/repairer has a higher level and is a top job (bold). This is because the top skills of the Conservator are more important to the elevator installer (as defined in the O*Net database) than to the electric meter installer.

Best Fit Jobs for Conservators (Providers and Protectors)

Job Title	Estimated Employment	Salary		
		Starting	Median	High
Electric Meter Installers and Repairers.	34,910	23,470	41,330	57,180
Gaugers.	31,230	28,220	45,180	57,040
First–Line Supervisors/Managers of Food Preparation and Serving Workers.	**624,180**	**14,870**	**22,680**	**37,740**
Rail–Track Laying and Maintenance Equipment Operators.	9,940	18,590	31,060	43,230
Gas Appliance Repairers.	33,910	17,300	28,860	45,750
Elevator Installers and Repairers.	**25,100**	**23,280**	**47,380**	**69,120**

Medical Records and Health Information Technicians.	**143,870**	**15,710**	**22,750**	**35,170**
Bus Drivers, Transit and Intercity.	175,470	15,890	25,710	41,660
Power Generating Plant Operators, Except Auxiliary Equipment Operators.	34,720	28,700	46,090	62,020
Electric Motor and Switch Assemblers and Repairers.	36,620	18,980	32,860	52,360
Electrical and Electronics Repairers, Powerhouse, Substation, and Relay.	19,300	30,760	48,540	60,320
Radio Mechanics.	7,110	19,540	32,990	53,290
Engine and Other Machine Assemblers.	66,090	16,800	28,010	44,680
Chemical Equipment Tenders.	**60,380**	**23,060**	**35,800**	**51,660**
First-Line Supervisors and Manager/Supervisors-Construction Trades Workers.	**502,010**	**28,660**	**44,790**	**70,780**

First–Line
Supervisors/Managers
of Mechanics,
Installers, and
Repairers. 421,740 26,860 44,250 70,090

**Food Service
Managers.** **282,290** **19,200** **31,720** **53,090**

Claims Examiners,
Property and Casualty
Insurance. 189,700 25,860 41,080 68,130

Librarians. 139,460 25,030 41,700 62,990

Financial Analysts. 159,490 31,880 52,420 101,760

Maintenance and
Repair Workers,
General. 1,216,250 16,320 27,850 44,570

Machinists. 420,320 18,740 30,740 45,430

Millwrights. 75,940 25,000 40,210 56,300

Municipal Fire
Fighting and
Prevention
Supervisors. 59,500 31,820 51,990 77,700

**Chemical Equipment
Controllers and
Operators.** **60,380** **23,060** **35,800** **51,660**

Boilermakers. 25,280 19,980 37,020 55,770

Metal Molding, Coremaking, and Casting Machine Operators and Tenders.	158,280	14,650	21,620	35,220
Riggers.	14,640	18,820	32,080	48,900
Model Makers, Metal and Plastic.	10,540	15,570	33,420	61,420
Elementary School Teachers, Except Special Education.	1,409,140	25,810	39,700	62,600
Forest Fire Fighting and Prevention Supervisors.	**59,500**	**31,820**	**51,990**	**77,700**
First-Line Supervisors, Customer Service.	**1,394,640**	**22,070**	**36,420**	**60,600**
Data Processing Equipment Repairers.	142,390	19,760	31,380	48,720
Police Patrol Officers.	571,210	23,790	39,790	58,900
Residential Advisors.	42,630	13,710	20,060	32,660
Special Education Teachers, Preschool, Kindergarten, and Elementary School.	208,970	26,640	40,880	66,210
Special Education Teachers, Middle School.	87,790	26,500	38,600	61,590

Special Education Teachers, Secondary School.	116,760	27,180	41,290	67,030
Directors, Religious Activities and Education.	13,610	13,850	27,000	50,600
Technical Directors/Managers.	**46,750**	**21,050**	**41,030**	**87,770**
Product Safety Engineers.	**42,800**	**34,710**	**54,630**	**82,320**
Air Traffic Controllers.	23,350	44,760	82,520	111,150
Nursing Instructors and Teachers, Postsecondary.	35,870	29,200	47,650	71,430
Highway Patrol Pilots.	571,210	23,790	39,790	58,900
Ship and Boat Captains.	21,080	23,280	47,510	73,090
Transportation Managers.	**116,680**	**31,470**	**54,230**	**90,730**
Adult Literacy, Remedial Education, and GED Teachers and Instructors.	53,250	19,700	33,540	59,280
Registered Nurses.	2,189,670	31,890	44,840	64,360
Program Directors.	**46,750**	**21,050**	**41,030**	**87,770**
Construction Managers.	**229,200**	**34,820**	**58,250**	**102,860**
Financial Managers, Branch or Department.	622,890	36,050	67,020	131,120

THE GUARDIAN ROLES

Fish and Game Wardens.	7,730	25,960	39,950	67,030
Dietitians and Nutritionists.	43,030	23,680	38,450	54,940
Industrial Production Managers.	**205,370**	**35,530**	**61,660**	**106,020**
Database Administrators.	108,000	29,400	51,990	89,320
Educational Psychologists.	103,120	28,090	48,320	76,840
First-Line Supervisors/Managers of Police and Detectives.	113,740	34,660	57,210	86,060
Medical and Public Health Social Workers.	103,390	22,490	34,790	53,160
Airframe-and-Power-Plant Mechanics.	135,730	25,080	40,550	56,100
Pilots, Ship.	**21,080**	**23,280**	**47,510**	**73,090**
Pharmacists.	**212,660**	**51,570**	**70,950**	**89,010**
Health Specialties Teachers, Postsecondary.	78,680	29,550	59,220	130,190
Computer Systems Analysts.	463,300	37,460	59,330	89,040
Engineering Managers.	242,280	52,350	84,070	130,350
Child, Family, and School Social Workers.	266,570	20,120	31,470	50,280

Aircraft Engine Specialists.	135,730	25,080	40,550	56,100
Physician Assistants.	55,490	32,690	61,910	88,100
Education Administrators, Postsecondary.	**92,280**	**32,650**	**59,480**	**109,280**
Computer Programmers.	530,730	35,020	57,590	93,210
Airline Pilots, Copilots, and Flight Engineers.	**94,820**	**36,110**	**110,940**	*
Postmasters and Mail Superintendents.	**26,850**	**35,380**	**44,260**	**64,960**
Administrative Law Judges, Adjudicators, and Hearing Officers.	12,560	32,970	61,240	111,590
Arbitrators, Mediators, and Conciliators.	4,850	23,360	43,060	93,170
Government Service Executives.	519,890	46,390	113,810	*
Clergy.	30,980	15,350	31,760	54,550
Industrial–Organizational Psychologists.	1,280	36,410	66,880	110,460
Mining and Geological Engineers, Including Mining Safety .Engineers.	6,690	36,070	60,820	100,050
Home Health Aides.	**561,120**	**12,770**	**17,120**	**24,810**

Computer Software Engineers, Applications.	374,640	42,710	67,670	106,680
Computer Software Engineers, Systems Software.	264,610	43,600	69,530	105,240
Curators.			*(no data available)*	
Epidemiologists.	2,480	31,070	48,390	78,630
Medical Scientists, Except Epidemiologists.	35,570	31,440	57,810	112,000
Podiatrists.	7,870	48,130	107,560	*
Criminal Investigators and Special Agents.	87,090	29,600	48,870	72,160
Licensed Practical and Licensed Vocational Nurses.	679,470	21,520	29,440	41,800
Veterinarians.	40,270	36,670	60,910	128,720
Psychiatrists.	21,280	50,930	118,640	*
Private Sector Executives.	519,890	46,390	113,810	*
Vocational Education Teachers Postsecondary.	115,080	21,840	38,170	65,610
Judges, Magistrate Judges, and .Magistrates.	25,190	19,320	86,760	134,660
Treasurers, Controllers, and Chief Financial Officers.	622,890	36,050	67,020	131,120

Family and General Practitioners.	132,620	44,970	114,170	*
Internists, General.	50,450	77,720	142,400	*
Obstetricians and Gynecologists.	18,240	98,490	*	*
Pediatricians, General.	25,580	77,980	125,970	*
Biologists.			*(no data available)*	
Geologists.	21,810	33,910	56,230	106,040
Lawyers.	**489,530**	**44,590**	**88,280**	*

*Indicates a salary greater than $145,000 per year.

Bold indicates this is a top job, based on both fit and/or total employment.

The jobs listed here are just the beginning. It is important to read through all the jobs for your temperament, and to browse the jobs for the other temperaments. This will ensure that you have identified your temperament correctly. Then, refer to chapter 12 for where to go from here.

CHAPTER 6

ARTISANS

I FIRST MET Brandon during an automotive lemon law case. Brandon was an expert witness for the plaintiff, even though he was only 30 years old. He works in his father's racing and tire shop, but his real passion is racing his own cars. He has been doing it since he was five years old, when his parents put him on a track in a shifter kart. Both his parents were racecar drivers, until they decided to open a racing shop. In the shop, Brandon is a suspension specialist, and knows all the tips and tricks required to make a car perform. He says he can tweak any car to perform better, taking into consideration such things as where and how the car will be driven all the way to how much the driver weighs in the car and how to balance that with the alignment and other adjustments.

It Takes All Types

What Brandon says he enjoys most about his job in the shop is the level of expertise he has at making adjustments to cars "by feel" rather than specification, getting that extra ounce of performance from them. Doing suspension work is a relatively physical activity, which Brandon enjoys. On the track, Brandon says "the rush and the competitiveness" are what he likes best. What he does not like is when he is rushed to complete a task, like the time a new engine did not arrive until the day before a race and he stayed up most of the night getting his car ready. He says when you are going 150 miles per hour, you really want to make sure everything is right. He also does not like routine, but says he gets plenty of challenge in the shop, where he works on everything from people's basic transportation to the high performance racecars he builds.

Brandon explained to me what it's like to race, which amounts to constant rush of data coming in very fast. It's like complete sensory input, followed by finely tuned output, to successfully operate the gas, brakes, steering, and shifting. During the race he must take into account how the tires are wearing by feel, how the engine is performing, the track conditions, the readings on the gauges, and of course, the other drivers and the tactics they are using. Brandon's success at professional racing comes naturally – he beat a track record at Malibu when he was 9 years old. Still, he works hard at racing and has corporate sponsors to help with the costs. Brandon says he never really considered any other job, but if he weren't racing, he says he'd probably be doing something with computers. It may not surprise you to learn that Brandon is an Artisan.

ARTISANS

People of the Artisan Temperament make up about 35% of the United States population. They are seen in many places, usually using their innate style – a sense of time, place and manner – to perform, entertain, enthrall with amazing feats, create, compose, and live life. This is how Artisans perceive themselves and how they like to be seen by others. They are clever, artistic, flexible, and optimistic. If Guardians are described as being the gravity that holds society together, then Artisans must be thought of as the comet streaking through in a blaze of light, not bound by a traditional orbit.

You probably have a picture of several Artisan coworkers already. They are the easy-going, practical, adaptable ones that will take risks others would not. Sometimes these risks are physically dangerous (as in the case of Brandon, an Artisan Performer), and sometimes they are risks that follow from the Artisan's desire for freedom to act on impulse, such as not following the rules and regulations. They may come to meetings late (or not at all), dress in a characteristic and non-traditional fashion, and always appear to be having fun doing whatever they are doing. These behaviors are not aimed to be insubordinate; but only to express the values Artisans hold to be free to choose and not to be tied down by what they perceive as unnecessary structure.

Not all Artisans are thrill seekers living life on the edge and looking for occupations that are as dangerous as they are exciting. Many Artisans are just that – artists – who use their skills with the medium they are working in to express themselves. These are the painters, sculptors, graphic and fashion designers, model makers, and music composers. They are also computer application and web designers, and mechanical and electrical engineers. But all Artisans do live – and live now! – to express themselves in the immediacy of the moment.

An expression of this artistic moment can be seen in the works of Frank Gehry, the famous Los Angeles architect, who exhibits the traits of an Artisan Composer much more than the typical career architect, the Rational Architect (Keirsey's role variant who he actually named after the profession). Gehry's work, embodied in buildings such the Gehry Residence in Santa Monica, California, the Guggenheim Museum in Bilbao, Spain, and the Experience Music Project in Seattle, Washington, practically eschews structure for composition. Whereas a Rational architect would be concerned with designing the structure to the specifications – fitting the required specifications in the most efficient, elegant, and permanent design, Gehry's designs barely appear as if they are solid in the present.

Gehry states, "I approach each building as a sculptural object, a spatial container, a space with light and air, a response to context and appropriateness of feeling and spirit. To this container, this sculpture, the user brings his baggage, his program, and interacts with it to accommodate his needs. If he can't do that, I've failed." In fact, Gehry has worked with artists and sculptors, especially early in his career before his current genius status was recognized. In an interview with *Architectural Record*, Gehry says,

So I felt at home with the artists and I learned a lot from them. I did some work for some of them....But I was intellectually intrigued with their process, their language, their attitudes, their ability to make things with their own hands. That it wasn't this detached thing. That it was hands-on and it was—there were a lot of things that felt more comfortable to me that way from the art world, and I became more and more detached from architecture, from the architecture world.

Artisans, Keirsey tells us, are concrete in their use of words. You can use this to spot Artisans in conversation, where they will talk about specifics rather than generalities, tend to be sincere and straightforward, but will often use hip and colorful expressions. They are very conscious of the sound of their spoken compositions. This fluency of language serves them well in carrying out their tactical roles.

Artisans display the tactical intelligence. Tactics is the art of working toward an immediate end – maneuvering to accomplish a goal – which Artisans excel at, especially when that goal is close at hand. They take on these goals, whether athletic competitions, games of skill, feats of daring, or a business negotiation (the "art of the deal") not only because it appeals to their nature to do so, but because they want to win. Through practice, the Artisan becomes ever more tactical, to the point where almost every situation and interaction is an opportunity for advantage, or a challenge not to lose relative position. This behavior can be seen in Artisans from racecar driver Brandon to the original deal artist, Donald Trump.

From an early age young Artisans are practicing their tactical skills, trusting their gut feelings and seeking out exciting situations where their adaptability can be put to use, usually along with their grace in motion.

Artisans are also utilitarian in their tool use. In practical terms, this means Artisans will employ what works when it works, and ignore that which is not immediately useful. As a consequence, the protocol and regulation so important to the Guardian is completely disregarded by the Artisan in pursuit of a goal. The goal itself – winning – is the desired result, not stability and security. Achieving this boldness, along with being clever, adaptable and artistic, increases the Artisan's self-image.

THE SELF-IMAGE OF ARTISANS

It is important to understand what makes up the self-image of ourselves and others if we are going to be able to effectively communicate, lead, follow, motivate, and appreciate each other in the workplace. Our self-image, according to Keirsey, is composed of three main attributes: self-esteem, self-respect, and self-confidence.

The self-esteem of Artisans is tied toward being artistic, graceful, and free. When they see themselves and are seen by others this way, they can increase their self-esteem. Because of this, Artisans are capable of practicing for long hours, honing their performance, skill, or art until perfected at that moment, even though the next performance or piece will be improvised on the spot. A successful act adds to their self-esteem, but a flub on stage or at the negotiation table will cause the Artisan great embarrassment.

Artisan self-respect comes from being bold, daring, and adventurous. To the Artisan, these traits imply fearlessness and courage. While this may result in many Artisans seeking death-defying experiences within their jobs (such as soldier, firefighter, or helicopter pilot), Artisans can gain this self-respect by "living dangerously" in such occupations as stand-up comic, emergency room doctor, or courtroom litigator. These jobs also require the courage to take risks. Consider Frank Gehry again, who risks his career, reputation, and the unflattering comments of his patrons with every design unveiling.

Self-confidence for Artisans is based on their ability to adapt. When Artisans feel free to respond to any situation that arises, they feel confident that they will be able to react, to express themselves, to employ the proper tactics, and to win. Because they are not bound by the codes, traditions, and confidence based on respectability (as the Guardians are), the Artisans are very successful at being adaptable, flexible, and dealing with any new problem or snafu that arises, doing so effectively through their utilitarian orientation; taking the risk without regard to the eventual consequences.

⚒ ⚒ ⚒

It Takes All Types

Archetype and Caricature

Keirsey presents General George S. Patton, Jr. as a prime example of the Artisan. A brilliant tactical leader, Patton was always ready to step into a difficult situation. Writing about the WWII invasion of North Africa, "Operation Torch," in his book *War As I Knew It*, Patton says:

> In forty hours I shall be in battle, with little information, and on the spur of the moment will have to make most momentous decisions, but I believe that one's spirit enlarges with responsibility and that, with God's help, I shall make them and make them right. It seems that my whole life has been pointed to this moment. When this job is done, I presume I will be pointed to the next step in the ladder of destiny. If I do my duty, the rest will take care of itself.

Patton's "whole life" is in the moment, with no greater strategic plan than this next battle during which he will make on-the-spot decisions using any available resources and his ability to grasp the battlefield in its entirety.

If Patton is the archetype of the Artisan, then archaeologist/adventure hero Indiana Jones from the movie *Raiders of the Lost Ark* is the ideal caricature. Indiana is constantly getting into and out of trouble and he uses his body and any other available tool – particularly his bullwhip – to assist in his escapes. In one characteristic scene, Indiana comes face-to-face with a sword-wielding assassin who shows his talent with his sword by flinging it around in a menacingly skillful display. Indiana knows his whip is no match but, as soon as the assassin finishes his swordplay, ready to finish Indiana next, Indiana pulls out his revolver and shoots the assassin. Tactical and utilitarian at their best.

Another example comes from the HBO series *Sex and the City*. The shows revolve around the lives of four women living in New York – each of whom embodies a different temperament. Samantha is the owner of her own successful public relations firm. She is bold and audacious, displaying an abundance of the traits that make up an Artisan Promoter. In one episode she attends a funeral for a fashion designer friend. The family asks that donations be sent to a charity. She says, "I'm going to help them raise money." Her friend says, "That's awfully nice of you." Samantha replies, "Forget nice, the mailing list will be priceless!" This is a typically Artisan view, ever on the lookout for the opportunity to increase her position.

MANAGING, LEADING, AND ENTREPRENEURSHIP

Artisans grasp the dynamics of an organization – how it works at the level of all the individual parts and people. They use this knowledge to find the weak points and to improve on them. They are very practical in this "troubleshooting," not trying to make broad sweeping changes, but economically making changes to personnel, policies, and procedures that will do the most good to improve individual outcomes. The Artisan's adaptability allows them to make these changes quickly and adapt to the new way of doing things. If these things turn out not to work well, the Artisan can quickly change position. They are seen as easy to work with by their colleagues, usually being perceived as friendly, funny and easy-going. Artisans create a sense of excitement within their organization, and this is often used to motivate their fellow managers and co-workers into action.

As entrepreneurs, Artisans display these same positive traits. They will proficiently assume the role of negotiator, crafting deals for the benefit of their enterprise. Again, Donald Trump is a prime example of the Artisan as entrepreneur. They are at their best when they are involved hands-on, either negotiating or trouble-shooting. If they lose this sense of excitement, they may become bored and lose interest in their endeavor. As a consequence, their colleagues may see Artisan leaders as unpredictable. Because they are generally not interested in greater abstractions and long-term strategic planning, the Artisan leader may not convey a sense of vision to colleagues and employees. However, given a concrete problem within an operation or a series of immediate challenges to overcome, the Artisan will strive to win – and often succeed.

Skills, Activities, Interests, and Values

In looking at career and job choices for the Artisans, we must consider the skills, activities, interests, and values of the person and the job. While your skills and interests may be different from other Artisans, the jobs presented have been shown to be those that interest a large portion of Artisans and that display skills that build naturally on the tactical intelligence. There is a range of activities and skill levels in the jobs presented in the next chapter, and the list is by no means exhaustive. It is meant to both illustrate the principles of finding a job that fits your temperament well and to point you in a series of directions for the skill level you have acquired or are willing to acquire.

Artisans' skills are developed through use and practice of the logistical intellect. These skills, in the job language of the Occupational Information Network (O*Net) sponsored by the U.S. Department of Labor, are:

THE SKILLS OF ARTISANS

- Persuasion
- Equipment Maintenance
- Problem Identification
- Speaking
- Troubleshooting
- Identification of Key Causes
- Repairing
- Installation
- Equipment Selection

These are the skills that were primarily used in assessing the skill component of the Artisan jobs. It is not necessarily that all of you display great aptitude in all these skills, but only that you recognize the ability to attain these skills through use will come more naturally to you. The jobs and careers presented in the next chapter will require some or all of these, and you can fill the bill by using your tactical intelligence.

There are 42 activities and over 100,000 activity entries for the 1100 jobs in the O*Net catalog. The top activities involved in the Artisan jobs are the following:

The Activities of Artisans
- Controlling Machines and Processes
- Handling and Moving Objects
- Repairing Mechanical Equipment
- Maintaining Mechanical Equipment
- Operating Vehicles or Equipment
- Identifying Objects, Actions, and Events
- Performing General Physical Activities
- Repairing Electrical Equipment
- Maintaining Electrical Equipment
- Selling or Influencing Others

These activities used in selecting jobs take full advantage of the Artisans' flexibility and adaptability, their artistic nature, a general physical orientation, and tactical intellect.

The next factors that went into determining the top jobs for Artisans were their interests, based on six well-defined interest areas. They are:

- *Realistic* - Are you interested in jobs that require athletic or mechanical ability, working with objects, machines, tools, plants or animals, or being outdoors?
- *Investigative* - Are you interested in jobs with people who like to observe, learn, investigate, analyze, evaluate or solve problems?
- *Artistic* - Are you interested in jobs involving artistic, innovative or intuitive abilities, and like to work in unstructured creative situations?
- *Social* - Do you like to work with people to inform, help, train, enlighten, develop or cure or are you skilled with words?
- *Enterprising* - Are you interested in jobs where you work with people to influence, perform, persuade, or lead for organizational goals or economic gain?
- *Conventional* - Are you interested in jobs that involve working with data, clerical tasks, or numerical ability, carrying things out in detail or following instructions?

Both the top interest areas and the order of their importance were used to filter good job matches for the Artisans.

Finally, a list of values appealing to Artisans was used to make sure that the jobs would match not only skills, activities, and interests, but key values. In fact, often the first thing you notice about another person is an expression of their values. For example, the top Artisan values are:

The Values of Artisans
- Ability Utilization
- Activity
- Creativity
- Autonomy
- Independence
- Achievement
- Compensation
- Social Status

If you have taken the Keirsey Temperament Sorter, and if the skills, activities and values above appeal to your sense of a job, then you are probably on the right track reading about Artisans. You should continue on to the next chapter with descriptions of Artisan roles and actual jobs. If not, please explore the chapters on the other three temperaments to find your ideal career.

CHAPTER 7

THE ARTISAN ROLES

ACCORDING TO temperament theory, Artisans tend toward one of two roles: Operator or Entertainer, which differ enough from each other that there is a separate list of jobs for each.

OPERATORS – THE PROMOTERS AND THE CRAFTERS

Operators are the action-oriented Artisans. They take on the role of expediting, through persuasion or the use of mechanisms, tools and other implements. They are *role directive*, which means that they are more apt to take charge and tell others what to do. They are the people who stand out in your mind when you picture a crisis and a few people are giving directions and shouting orders. Operators come in two role variants – Promoters and Crafters –

both of which share the tough-minded, directive traits. Myers referred to the Promoter as the ESTP and the Crafter as the ISTP.

As the name suggests, Promoters tend to be more expressive. They work in any cause that requires the promotion of their agenda. Promoters can influence, convince, publicize, negotiate, and deal. In contrast, Crafters are more reserved, working less with the people in an organization and more with the actual tools and implements, aware of the resources at their disposal and conditions at hand.

When not satisfied in their current career, or when looking for a new career, Operators focus on the many experiences they have had. They seek new positions that will let them continue to have varied and satisfying challenges, rather than routine repeat experiences. For example, the following are typical Operator reactions to job changes:

> My technical background is in finance, software, and quantitative modeling. I've been managing for 2 years now. I've owned three companies in the past, but they were small businesses.

✂ ✂ ✂

> I've recently been laid off from a tech company and feel that its time to get back on course. I have a computer science degree and had been a software engineer 10 years ago. For obvious reasons I became stir crazy and moved into the services and sales support end of the business. Anyway the last 6 years I have been in management and the farther I

got away from being able to do the same job as my people the more unsatisfied and unmotivated I'd become. Not to mention my technology skills are now very dated. So my dilemma is this: I could look for a line manager job at a new company, but I would be stuck in my rut if I did this. I am torn between finding a totally new career and getting my tech skills upgraded. Are there any non-tech fields that are more natural for someone with my background?

JOBS FOR OPERATORS

The jobs listed on the next pages are top matches for Operators, but by no means the only careers you should consider. Listed next to each standard job classification are the total number of people employed in that occupation in the United States and the salary ranges. The "starting" salary is the number that 90% of people in that job earn more than. The "high" salary is the number that 90% of people in that job earn less than. So 80% of the people in a job earn between the starting and high salary figures. The "median" is the number that half the people earn more than and half earn less than. These are national averages, and you could earn more or less.

The jobs in bold are the "best of the best" for your temperament and role. These are based on the degree to which the job fit your personality and also the number of available jobs, relative to the amount of people of your temperament in the population. For example, Forest Fire Fighting and Prevention

Supervisor would be a good job for an Operator, but with only about 1,000 positions available nationwide, it would not be as helpful to list it as a top job. However, it helps to list it because the skill might be similar to another job you are considering, or it may point you in a direction that you would otherwise have missed.

Finally, the jobs are in rough order from the lowest skill level *for the skills required of the job* to the highest level. For example, electric motor and switch assembler and repairer is the first job listed, and so would have a lower "level" than electrician. Both jobs would seem roughly equivalent, yet electrician has a higher level and is a top job (bold). This is because the top skills of the Operator are more important to the electrician job (as defined in the O*Net database) than to the electric motor and switch assembler and repairer.

Best Fit Jobs for Operators (Promoters and Crafters)

Job Title	Estimated Employment	Salary		
		Starting	Median	High
Electric Motor and Switch Assemblers and Repairers.	36,620	18,980	32,860	52,360
Electrical and Electronics Repairers, Powerhouse, Substation, and Relay.	19,300	30,760	48,540	60,320

Engine and Other Machine Assemblers.	66,090	16,800	28,010	44,680
Tool Grinders, Filers, and Sharpeners.	28,360	17,480	27,510	45,890
Maintenance Workers, Machinery.	107,500	19,150	30,970	47,310
Semiconductor Processors.	**67,000**	**18,410**	**25,430**	**39,720**
Cooling and Freezing Equipment Operators and Tenders.	7,410	13,570	20,180	34,140
Maintenance and Repair Workers, General.	1,216,250	16,320	27,850	44,570
Electrical Power–Line Installers and Repairers.	96,200	25,710	45,780	63,130
Machinists.	420,320	18,740	30,740	45,430
Millwrights.	75,940	25,000	40,210	56,300
Boilermakers.	25,280	19,980	37,020	55,770
Industrial Machinery Mechanics.	192,180	23,530	35,980	54,620
Metal Molding, Coremaking, and Casting Machine Operators and Tenders.	158,280	14,650	21,620	35,220
Art Directors.	20,560	30,130	56,880	109,440
Riggers.	14,640	18,820	32,080	48,900

Model Makers, Metal and Plastic.	10,540	15,570	33,420	61,420
Fitness Trainers and Aerobics Instructors.	157,230	13,150	22,790	54,030
Municipal Fire Fighting and Prevention Supervisors.	59,500	31,820	51,990	77,700
Watch Repairers.	4,000	13,480	25,130	43,590
Computer and Information Systems Managers.	**283,480**	**44,090**	**78,830**	**127,460**
Forest Fire Fighting and Prevention Supervisors.	59,500	31,820	51,990	77,700
Travel Clerks.	**199,700**	**15,650**	**22,620**	**42,570**
Forest Fire Inspectors and Prevention Specialists.	1,040	17,060	32,140	50,680
Fire Investigators	**11,900**	**24,790**	**41,630**	**65,030**
Credit Analysts.	63,420	24,220	40,180	72,880
Combination Machine Tool Setters and Set-Up Operators, Metal and Plastic.	109,950	17,080	26,960	48,430
Medical and Clinical Laboratory Technologists.	144,530	29,240	40,510	55,560
Electricians.	**640,260**	**23,530**	**40,120**	**65,960**
Wholesale and Retail	**137,040**	**21,570**	**37,200**	**70,750**

Buyers, Except Farm Products.			
Police Patrol Officers.	**571,210**	**23,790**	**39,790**	**58,900**
Food Service Managers.	**282,290**	**19,200**	**31,720**	**53,090**
Industrial Engineering Technicians.	65,220	25,860	40,910	70,240
Forensic Science Technicians.	6,150	23,890	37,520	58,510
Insurance Adjusters, Examiners, and Investigators.	**189,700**	**25,860**	**41,080**	**68,130**
First–Line Supervisors/Managers of Police and Detectives.	113,740	34,660	57,210	86,060
Zoologists and Wildlife Biologists.	11,710	27,140	43,980	68,190
Sales Agents, Securities and Commodities.	269,310	24,770	56,080	*
Personnel Recruiters.	188,060	22,520	36,480	71,040
Sales Representatives, Wholesale and Manufacturing, Except Technical and Scientific Products.	1,379,860	21,450	40,340	82,830
Product Safety Engineers.	42,800	34,710	54,630	82,320

Communication Equipment Mechanics, Installers, and Repairers.	192,470	25,050	44,030	56,630
Agents and Business Managers of Artists, Performers, and Athletes.	6,600	20,810	57,040	*
Directors, Religious Activities and Education.	13,610	13,850	27,000	50,600
Sales Representatives, Mechanical Equipment and Supplies.	373,630	27,450	52,620	102,000
Real Estate Sales Agents.	**108,880**	**14,460**	**27,640**	**78,540**
Directors– Stage, Motion Pictures, Television, and Radio.	**46,750**	**21,050**	**41,030**	**87,770**
Sales Agents, Financial Services.	269,310	24,770	56,080	*
Marketing Managers.	202,100	35,950	71,240	133,300
Talent Directors.	46,750	21,050	41,030	87,770
Technical Writers.	50,700	28,890	47,790	74,360
Airline Pilots, Copilots, and Flight Engineers.	94,820	36,110	110,940	*
Commercial Pilots.	18,040	24,290	43,300	92,000

THE ARTISAN ROLES

Child Support, Missing Persons, and Unemployment Insurance Fraud Investigators.	87,090	29,600	48,870	72,160
Property, Real Estate, and Community Association Managers.	145,340	16,720	36,020	80,360
Chiropractors.	**16,740**	**22,910**	**67,030**	*****
Market Research Analysts.	**99,030**	**27,570**	**51,190**	**96,360**
Health Educators.	**43,670**	**20,150**	**33,860**	**57,430**
Emergency Medical Technicians and Paramedics.	165,530	14,660	22,460	37,760
Natural Sciences Managers.	38,870	43,110	75,880	128,090
Food Scientists and Technologists.			*(no data available)*	
Chemical Engineers.	31,530	45,200	65,960	93,430
Mining and Geological Engineers, Including Mining Safety Engineers.	6,690	36,070	60,820	100,050
Probation Officers and Correctional Treatment Specialists.	80,500	25,010	38,150	59,010

Radio and Television Announcers.			*(no data available)*
Advertising Sales Agents.	151,140	18,570	35,850	87,240
Insurance Sales Agents.	240,830	20070	38750	91530
Sales Managers.	344,180	34,700	68,520	137,780
Aerospace Engineering and Operations Technicians.	19,850	33,090	48,600	69,700
Animal Scientists.			*(no data available)*
Industrial Safety and Health Engineers.	42,800	34,710	54,630	82,320
Materials Inspectors.	571,220	15,250	25,420	46,200
Reporters and Correspondents.			*(no data available)*
Highway Patrol Pilots.	571,210	23,790	39,790	58,900
Producers.	46,750	21,050	41,030	87,770
Optometrists.	23,880	40,450	82,860	*
Computer Support Specialists.	522,570	21,260	36,460	63,480
Soil Conservationists.	12,980	30,240	47,140	68,300
Agricultural Crop Farm Managers.	5,370	20,940	38,400	75,420
Marine Engineers.	4,680	35,640	60,890	89,760
Electronics Engineering Technicians.	244,570	25,210	40,020	58,320

Network Systems and Data Communications Analysts.	119,220	33,360	54,510	88,620
Industrial Engineers.	171,810	38,140	58,580	86,370
Hydrologists.	7,240	35,910	55,410	85,260
Agricultural Engineers.	2,170	33,660	55,850	91,600
Public Relations Specialists.	128,570	22,780	39,580	70,480
Private Sector Executives.	519,890	46,390	113,810	*
Geologists.	21,810	33,910	56,230	106,040
Advertising and Promotions Managers.	93,420	27,840	53,360	119,310
Education Administrators, Postsecondary.	92,280	32,650	59,480	109,280
Anesthesiologists.	24,350	88,170	*	*
Obstetricians and Gynecologists.	18,240	98,490	*	*
Chemists.	82,320	29620	50080	88030
Electrical and Electronics Repairers, Commercial and Industrial Equipment.	81,760	22,670	36,910	53,620
Lawyers.	489,530	44590	88280	*
Aerospace Engineers.	71,550	47,700	67,930	94,310
Nuclear Engineers.	12,610	58,030	79,360	105,930

Sales Engineers.	**88,240**	**33,930**	**56,520**	**95,560**
Veterinarians.	40,270	36,670	60,910	128,720
Computer Programmers.	530,730	35,020	57,590	93,210
Computer Software Engineers, Applications.	374,640	42,710	67,670	106,680
Computer Hardware Engineers.	63,680	42,620	67,300	107,360

*Indicates a salary greater than $145,000 per year.

Bold indicates this is a top job, based on both fit and/or total employment.

The jobs listed here are just the beginning. It is important to read through all the jobs for your temperament, and to browse the jobs for the other temperaments. This will ensure that you have identified your temperament correctly. Then, refer to chapter 12 for where to go from here.

ENTERTAINERS – THE PERFORMERS AND THE COMPOSERS

Entertainers are the improvisational Artisans. They take on the role of entertaining, usually by sharing their creations with others. These creations are usually devised or composed spontaneously, without planning but with a lot of creative improvisation. They are *role informative*, which means that they are less apt to take charge and tell others what to do. Entertainers come in two role variants –

Performers and Composers – both of which share the tender-minded, informative traits. Myers referred to the Performer as the ESFP and the Composer as the ISFP.

Performers tend to be more expressive. They are the people you would imagine on stage, in front of a crowd, displaying and demonstrating their skills. Crafters are more reserved, preferring to be the creative behind the curtain rather than in front of it, directing, designing, writing, and decorating.

When not satisfied in their current career, or when looking for a new career, Entertainers look to make a dramatic change. They seek new careers and jobs that may be totally unrelated to their current position or training, rather than trying to build on their past experiences. For example, the following are typical Entertainer reactions to job changes:

> I have been a computer technician for the past 5 years in our local school district. I am basically self-taught (no formal schooling or certifications) and enjoy learning about how to fix computers by actually doing it. I especially like challenging and complex problems that need to be addressed. I feel energized when I resolve these issues. I have recently taken a part time sales job on the weekends at a local winery. I never thought of myself as a salesperson, but I absolutely love dealing with customers and have a real desire to get them to enjoy the wine they taste and then buy it! I wonder if I should pursue a career in sales full

time. I like working independently, but really enjoy meeting new people.

✺ ✺ ✺

I began my career in communications in the newsroom as a copy editor, but after two years tired of the bad hours, the sameness of each day and the lack of creativity required from my job. I made the switch to public relations and I found the perfect field that allowed me to use my organizational and analytical skills and flex my creative muscle. Best of all, the field requires lots of writing, which is my passion.

Jobs for Entertainers

The jobs listed on the next pages are top matches for Entertainers, but by no means the only careers you should consider. Listed next to each standard job classification are the total number of people employed in that occupation in the United States and the salary ranges. The "starting" salary is the number that 90% of people in that job earn more than. The "high" salary is the number that 90% of people in that job earn less than. So 80% of the people in a job earn between the starting and high salary figures. The "median" is the number that half the people earn more than and half earn less than. These are national averages, and you could earn more or less.

94

THE ARTISAN ROLES

The jobs in bold are the "best of the best" for your temperament and role. These are based on the degree to which the job fit your personality and also the number of available jobs, relative to the amount of people of your temperament in the population. For example, Agricultural Engineer would be a good job for an Entertainer, but with only about 2,000 positions available nationwide, it would not be as helpful to list it as a top job. However, it helps to list it because the skill might be similar to another job you are considering, or it may point you in a direction that you would otherwise have missed.

Finally, the jobs are in rough order from the lowest skill level *for the skills required of the job* to the highest level. For example, electric motor and switch assembler and repairer is the first job listed, and so would have a lower "level" than electrician. Both jobs would seem roughly equivalent, yet electrician has a higher level and is a top job (bold). This is because the top skills of the Entertainer are more important to the electrician job (as defined in the O*Net database) than to the electric motor and switch assembler and repairer.

Best Fit Jobs for Entertainers (Performers and Composers)

Job Title	Estimated Employment	Salary		
		Starting	Median	High
Electric Motor and Switch Assemblers and Repairers.	36,620	18,980	32,860	52,360

Electrical and Electronics Repairers, Powerhouse, Substation, and Relay.	19,300	30,760	48,540	60,320
Engine and Other Machine Assemblers.	66,090	16,800	28,010	44,680
Tool Grinders, Filers, and Sharpeners.	28,360	17,480	27,510	45,890
Maintenance Workers, Machinery.	107,500	19,150	30,970	47,310
Semiconductor Processors.	**67,000**	**18,410**	**25,430**	**39,720**
Cooling and Freezing Equipment Operators and Tenders.	7,410	13,570	20,180	34,140
Maintenance and Repair Workers, General.	1,216,250	16,320	27,850	44,570
Electrical Power–Line Installers and Repairers.	96,200	25,710	45,780	63,130
Machinists.	420,320	18,740	30,740	45,430
Millwrights.	75,940	25,000	40,210	56,300
Boilermakers.	**25,280**	**19,980**	**37,020**	**55,770**
Industrial Machinery Mechanics.	192,180	23,530	35,980	54,620

Metal Molding, Coremaking, and Casting Machine Operators and Tenders.	158,280	14,650	21,620	35,220
Art Directors.	20,560	30,130	56,880	109,440
Riggers.	14,640	18,820	32,080	48,900
Model Makers, Metal and Plastic.	10,540	15,570	33,420	61,420
Fitness Trainers and Aerobics Instructors.	157,230	13,150	22,790	54,030
Fine Artists, Including Painters, Sculptors, and Illustrators.	**11,930**	**14,690**	**31,190**	**58,580**
Municipal Fire Fighting and Prevention Supervisors.	59,500	31,820	51,990	77,700
Set Designers.	8,470	13,820	31,440	57,400
Watch Repairers.	4,000	13,480	25,130	43,590
Anesthesiologists.	24,350	88,170	*	*
Fashion Designers.	10,460	24,710	48,530	103,970
Computer and Information Systems Managers.	283,480	44,090	78,830	127,460
Chefs and Head Cooks.	**122,860**	**15,380**	**25,110**	**47,350**
Registered Nurses.	2,189,670	31,890	44,840	64,360

Forest Fire Fighting and Prevention Supervisors.	59,500	31,820	51,990	77,700
Travel Clerks.	**199,700**	**15,650**	**22,620**	**42,570**
Forest Fire Inspectors and Prevention Specialists.	1,040	17,060	32,140	50,680
Fire Investigators.	**11,900**	**24,790**	**41,630**	**65,030**
Combination Machine Tool Setters and Set-Up Operators, Metal and Plastic.	**109,950**	**17,080**	**26,960**	**48,430**
Medical and Clinical Laboratory Technologists.	144,530	29,240	40,510	55,560
Electricians.	**640,260**	**23,530**	**40,120**	**65,960**
Wholesale and Retail Buyers, Except Farm Products.	**137,040**	**21,570**	**37,200**	**70,750**
Food Service Managers.	**282,290**	**19,200**	**31,720**	**53,090**
Vocational Education Teachers, Middle School.	19,010	27,040	39,330	57,590
Vocational Education Teachers, Secondary School.	103,200	28,460	42,080	61,580
Industrial Engineering Technicians.	65,220	25,860	40,910	70,240

Dietitians and Nutritionists.	43,030	23,680	38,450	54,940
Insurance Adjusters, Examiners, and Investigators.	**189,700**	**25,860**	**41,080**	**68,130**
First–Line Supervisors/Managers of Police and Detectives.	113,740	34,660	57,210	86,060
Zoologists and Wildlife Biologists.	11,710	27,140	43,980	68,190
Sales Agents, Securities and Commodities.	269,310	24,770	56,080	*
Farm and Home Management Advisors.	**10,290**	**17,940**	**36,290**	**61,580**
Personnel Recruiters.	**188,060**	**22,520**	**36,480**	**71,040**
Sales Representatives, Wholesale and Manufacturing, Except Technical and Scientific Products.	1,379,860	21,450	40,340	82,830
Product Safety Engineers.	42,800	34,710	54,630	82,320
Communication Equipment Mechanics, Installers, and Repairers.	**192,470**	**25,050**	**44,030**	**56,630**

Agents and Business Managers of Artists, Performers, and Athletes.	6,600	20,810	57,040	*
Sales Representatives, Mechanical Equipment and Supplies.	373,630	27,450	52,620	102,000
Real Estate Sales Agents.	**108,880**	**14,460**	**27,640**	**78,540**
Directors– Stage, Motion Pictures, Television, and Radio.	**46,750**	**21,050**	**41,030**	**87,770**
Sales Agents, Financial Services.	269,310	24,770	56,080	*
Substance Abuse and Behavioral Disorder Counselors.	56,080	18,850	28,510	43,210
Mental Health and Substance Abuse Social Workers.	79,740	19,300	30,170	48,750
Marketing Managers.	202,100	35,950	71,240	133,300
Talent Directors.	46,750	21,050	41,030	87,770
Airline Pilots, Copilots, and Flight Engineers.	94,820	36,110	110,940	*
Child Support, Missing Persons, and Unemployment Insurance Fraud Investigators.	87,090	29,600	48,870	72,160
Self-Enrichment Education Teachers.	125,960	14480	27960	52790

THE ARTISAN ROLES

Chiropractors.	16,740	22,910	67,030	*
Market Research Analysts.	99,030	27,570	51,190	96,360
Health Educators.	43,670	20,150	33,860	57,430
Social and Community Service Managers.	93,460	23450	39130	67920
Emergency Medical Technicians and Paramedics.	165,530	14,660	22,460	37,760
Probation Officers and Correctional Treatment Specialists.	80,500	25010	38150	59010
Radio and Television Announcers.			*(no data available)*	
Advertising Sales Agents.	151,140	18,570	35,850	87,240
Insurance Sales Agents.	240,830	20070	38750	91530
Sales Managers.	344,180	34,700	68,520	137,780
Animal Scientists.			*(no data available)*	
Child, Family, and School Social Workers.	266,570	20120	31470	50280
Industrial Safety and Health Engineers.	42,800	34,710	54,630	82,320
Materials Inspectors.	571,220	15,250	25,420	46,200
Reporters and Correspondents.			*(no data available)*	
Highway Patrol Pilots.	571,210	23,790	39,790	58,900
Producers.	46,750	21,050	41,030	87,770

Computer Support Specialists.	522,570	21,260	36,460	63,480
Agricultural Crop Farm Managers.	5,370	20,940	38,400	75,420
Electronics Engineering Technicians.	**244,570**	**25,210**	**40,020**	**58,320**
Network Systems and Data Communications Analysts.	**119,220**	**33,360**	**54,510**	**88,620**
Industrial Engineers.	171,810	38,140	58,580	86,370
Hydrologists.	**7,240**	**35,910**	**55,410**	**85,260**
Agricultural Engineers.	2,170	33,660	55,850	91,600
Public Relations Specialists.	128,570	22,780	39,580	70,480
Private Sector Executives.	519,890	46,390	113,810	*
Nursing Instructors and Teachers, Postsecondary.	35,870	29,200	47,650	71,430
Advertising and Promotions Managers.	93,420	27,840	53,360	119,310
Education Administrators, Postsecondary.	92,280	32,650	59,480	109,280
Family and General Practitioners.	**132,620**	**44,970**	**114,170**	*

Obstetricians and Gynecologists.	18,240	98,490	*	*
Pediatricians, General.	25,580	77980	125970	*
Electrical and Electronics Repairers, Commercial and Industrial Equipment.	81,760	22,670	36,910	53,620
Lawyers.	**489,530**	**44590**	**88280**	*
Aerospace Engineers.	71,550	47,700	67,930	94,310
Sales Engineers.	**88,240**	**33,930**	**56,520**	**95,560**
Veterinarians.	40,270	36,670	60,910	128,720
Computer Programmers.	530,730	35,020	57,590	93,210
Computer Systems Analysts.	463,300	37,460	59,330	89,040
Computer Software Engineers, Applications.	374,640	42,710	67,670	106,680

*Indicates a salary greater than $145,000 per year.

Bold indicates this is a top job, based on both fit and/or total employment.

It Takes All Types

The jobs listed here are just the beginning. It is important to read through all the jobs for your temperament, and to browse the jobs for the other temperaments. This will ensure that you have identified your temperament correctly. Then, refer to chapter 12 for where to go from here.

CHAPTER 8

IDEALISTS

KATHRYN WENT TO COLLEGE with the idea of becoming a history major, like her three siblings. When the time came to declare a major, she did not pick history, but instead chose sociology. She says, "It was about people. My first class in sociology was so much more fascinating than any other class I had taken, since it was about how people are affected by societal forces – family, race, gender, class – that shape who we are." After Kathryn's graduation, she really didn't know what she wanted to do. So many things were interesting to her on an intellectual level, but not many of them fit her idea of 40 hours a week. Still, she needed to work, so she went to an employment agency and told the agent, "I want to work for a non-profit, something with people, but not really anything 'corporate'."

105

The employment agency apparently understood what Kathryn was looking for, and placed her with a national land conservation group that concentrated on preserving land for the use of people. While there, Kathryn worked as a legal secretary and an administrative assistant to the executive vice president. However, her real function seemed to be as a mentor to the other employees she worked with. Her cubicle was a meeting place for her compatriots, and not merely because it was close to the network printer. People came to her to express their joys, frustrations, desires and dilemmas. They were sure to get support from Kathryn, who has a talent for drawing out the best in people.

While Kathryn believed in the cause she was working for and was quite competent at the duties listed in her job descriptions, those tasks took a back seat to real job she undertook: rallying the troops, listening to their problems, and encouraging them to do what she and they both knew they were capable of achieving. The tasks in her job description sometimes bored Kathryn, but the real stress for her came from bearing the weight of others' problems, which she sometimes took upon herself with characteristic empathy. In the end, Kathryn left to start a family, but she maintains close relationships with many of the people she met, and even those she does not remain in contact with remember her fondly. Kathryn, if you have not guessed, fits the temperament profile of the Idealist.

People of the Idealist Temperament make up 10-15% of the United States population. They are relatively scarce, but both identifiable and necessary. If Guardians are the glue that binds society together, then Idealists must be viewed as the lubricant that permits society to function without building up too much friction. The Idealist is constantly concerned with self-development and authenticity, both for themselves and others. They cannot bear to think that they are not being true to themselves, and it bothers them just as much to learn that someone else is not being true to his or her values, even if those values are different – or even contradictory – to the Idealists'.

Surely the slogan "Think globally, act locally" applies first and foremost to the Idealist. They see the relationships that exist everywhere, and they transform these into action in the workplace, although what that action will be cannot be predicted. Idealists often translate this universal view into the workplace by seeing the potential in the people around them. They will mentor, counsel, and strive to create harmony in their work setting, whether within their job description, or not. These tasks are often found in the Idealists' job descriptions, since human resources departments and other advocate positions frequently abound with people of this temperament. They are also found in positions requiring creativity in dealing with people, such as artist, therapist, counselor, and teacher.

Keirsey tells us that the Idealists are abstract in their use of words. You can use this to spot Idealists in conversation, where they will bring forth great abstractions on love, hate, life and death, using metaphors to link their abstractions to the things and people they are describing. "I hate this; I love that; That product is the worst; Her work is absolutely the best." The person or thing they are speaking of becomes the abstraction, even though this is usually an exaggeration. This is in contrast to the Guardians and Artisans, who display concrete word usage, or the Rationals who display abstract word usage, but who, rather than exaggerate, tend to qualify and understate their expressions.

According to Keirsey, Idealists display the diplomatic intelligence. Diplomacy is a sensitivity towards others' feelings, which translates into a way of dealing with others that tends to improve relationships and create harmony. This innate empathy the Idealists display seems to be present from an early age, and becomes more natural in their everyday interactions and through practice. Remember my daughter who as an infant would become saddened at the sound of other children crying. As a six-year old, she seems to strive for harmony and will offer defenses for any underdog or otherwise maligned person, trying to create a bridge between actions that are perceived as negative and actions that have a good intent. For example, I commented once in the car about someone driving too slowly, frustration in my voice. She responded, "Maybe they just don't know their way around our neighborhood, like we do." For Idealists, everyone is truly equal, which means to them that everyone is alike in being worthy of attention, trust, and respect.

Idealists are also cooperative in their tool use. However, Idealists are also the least interested in the actual use of tools. In the broader sense of the word, almost everything physical around us is a tool: our homes are tools for protection from the elements, cars are tools for moving ourselves, streets tools for carrying cars, and so on. Whereas to the Guardian, these things need regulations and rules to govern their proper use, to the Idealist they do not take the tool as a given in the first place. While the Guardian says "Here is a car, how shall we regulate its speed?", the Idealists says "Do we all agree we want cars?" The cooperative agreement on the use of the tool that gives comfort to the Idealist is the consensus surrounding the use of the tool in the first place, while the (concrete) Guardian accepts the existence of the tool, and is cooperative in the rules that govern its use.

As they enter the workforce, Idealists are often at a loss to apply their diplomatic intelligence to the needs of employers, as expressed in the job descriptions employers write. Idealists look at the description and the tasks laid out and do not see anything appealing or of value to them. Hence, they have a hard time finding a job or career that they believe will suit them. However, once they actually take a position, Idealists often find that the job description is secondary to the people needs of the organization. They recognize that the tasks of the job must be completed, which they can and will do, but they view their real job as mentoring and advocating for their colleagues and customers. Idealists also have a sense of what might be, and they bring this future orientation with them into the workplace in a creative and meaningful way. It is when Idealists can explore these possibilities, either within the role of their explicit duties or by creating potential within those around them, that they will increase their self-image.

It Takes All Types

The Self-Image of Idealists

It is important to understand what makes up the self-image of ourselves and others if we are going to be able to effectively communicate, lead, follow, motivate, and appreciate each other in the workplace. Our self-image, according to Keirsey, is composed of three main attributes: self-esteem, self-respect, and self-confidence.

The self-esteem of Idealists is tied toward feeling connected with others in an empathetic way. When they see themselves and are seen by others this way, they can increase their self-esteem. Because of this, Idealists are usually very available to others, especially when the other person is going through an emotional crisis. Being there, and being perceived as someone who is there and connected, increases the Idealist's self-esteem. At the same time, these initial encounters and empathetic feelings may not always last, causing the Idealist to move on to the next person with whom a connection can be made.

Self-respect for an Idealist comes from a sense that they have good intentions toward others. They cannot bear to harbor bad thoughts about others, and do not enjoy hearing tales of the ill in the world. This makes Idealists ideally suited for the tasks they take on in their careers, either explicitly or by nature. As an advocate or mentor, their job is to be the voice that speaks for the good of the person and to assist the individual in becoming the best they can and in living up to their full potential.

IDEALISTS

Self-confidence for Idealists arises from authenticity. If an Idealist feels he is not being true to himself, he cannot feel confident in what he is doing. He will experience self-doubt until he discovers his true nature. Idealists may also feel that others are watching them and viewing their actions as inauthentic – passing judgment on them. Idealists want to please others and be seen as meeting the goals and standards set by those around them. These feelings, while often hypersensitive and unfounded, can actually prevent the Idealist from being authentic. On one hand, they seek the approval for their actions from others, and on the other, they seek an integrity that comes from individual authenticity.

ARCHETYPE AND CARICATURE

Mohandas Gandhi, the non-violent leader of the Indian nationalist movement, is a prime example of an Idealist. Idealists are focused on bringing together, including, and developing people. They are always focused on the individual truths within themselves and others. In Gandhi's autobiography, also titled "My Experiments with Truth," he writes, "The highest honour that my friends can do me is to enforce in their own lives the programme that I stand for or to resist me to their utmost if they do not believe in it." Here the paradox of believing and striving for transformation for oneself and also desiring others to express their truth is clearly seen.

If Gandhi is the archetype of the Idealist, then Stuart Smalley, *Saturday Night Live*'s fictional host of cable access show "Daily

Affirmations," is the perfect caricature. "Stuart Smalley is a caring nurturer, a member of several twelve-step programs, but not a licensed therapist," the show's announcer states. Stuart (played by comedian Al Franken) spends most of each show reaffirming that he and his audience is "good enough," "smart enough, and that "people like me." Through Smalley, Franken pokes fun at several transformative fads, such as anger management, sensitivity training, and self-help programs for people who are always "becoming" but never get there. Of course, for the Idealist, there is no "there," except the journey.

Another example comes from the HBO series *Sex and the City*. The show revolves around the lives of four women living in New York – each of whom seems to embody a different temperament. Carrie Bradshaw is the writer in the show who pens the 'Sex and the City" column, using the foursome's experiences for inspiration. She exemplifies the constant self-examination and searching for the answers to the complicated questions of relationships and life. At the end of one episode, tapping out her column, she writes:

> Women can be anything they want – an astronaut, the head of an Internet company, a stay-at-home mom....There are no rules anymore. The choices are endless, and can be delivered right to your door. But have we become so spoiled by choices that we're unable to make one? Can we have it all?

✵ ✵ ✵

IDEALISTS

MANAGING, LEADING, AND ENTREPRENEURSHIP

Idealists create harmony in an organization, but as leaders they also serve to change their colleagues and subordinates into the best people they can be. Their skill at bringing out the best in people is natural and positive. They usually accomplish this task through their gifted speaking ability, by listening to others, and by truly caring about employees' career and personal development. The Idealist manager excels at soliciting opinions and ideas from everyone on the team, building a plan through the consensus of all. Idealists are also excellent spokespeople for an idea or vision, as long as they believe in it, and they can easily use their gift for language to convey that vision to others.

As entrepreneurs, Idealists display these same positive traits. They can turn an imaginative dream into a reality by creating a people-centered organization that brings out the best in every individual. They do this by creating work environments that are free from bureaucracy and competition between coworkers and that rely on a commitment to a goal or ideal. Respect and caring for each other is also a requirement of an Idealist entrepreneur's workplace. In practice, the Idealist leader will not be very hands-on, preferring to let the employee develop out the position in their own expressive way, as long as the desired end is met in a way that complies with the Idealist's standards for quality and integrity. At times, this can lead to abandonment by the Idealist of needed managerial duties in favor of more exploration. Often, Idealist leaders greatest achievement is walking this fine line between recognizing that some people provide greater contributions in certain areas than others, while at the same time creating a sense that everyone is on the same team.

Skills, Activities, Interests, and Values

In looking at career and job choices for the Idealists, we must consider the skills, activities, interests, and values of the person and the job. While your skills and interests may be different from other Idealists, the jobs presented have been shown to be those that interest a large portion of Idealists and that display skills that build naturally on the diplomatic intelligence. There is a range of activities and skill levels in the jobs presented in the next chapter, and the list is by no means exhaustive. It is meant to both illustrate the principles of finding a job that fits your temperament well and to point you in a series of directions for the skill level you have acquired or are willing to acquire.

Idealists' skills are developed through use and practice of the diplomatic intellect. These skills, in the job language of the Occupational Information Network (O*Net) sponsored by the U.S. Department of Labor, are:

The Skills of Idealists
- Active Listening
- Reading Comprehension

- Writing
- Social Perceptiveness
- Instructing
- Information Gathering
- Idea Evaluation
- Visioning
- Synthesis/Reorganization
- Learning Strategies
- Active Learning
- Idea Generation
- Systems Perception

These are the skills that were primarily used in assessing the skill component of the Idealist jobs. It is not necessarily that all of you display great aptitude in all these skills, but only that you recognize the ability to attain these skills through use will come more naturally to you. The jobs and careers presented in the next chapter will require some or all of these, and you can fill the bill by using your diplomatic intelligence.

There are 42 activities and over 100,000 activity entries for the 1100 jobs in the O*Net catalog. The top activities involved in the Idealist jobs are the following:

THE ACTIVITIES OF IDEALISTS
- Communicating With Persons Outside The Organization
- Communicating With Other Workers

- Guiding, Directing, & Motivating Subordinates
- Teaching Others
- Thinking Creatively
- Establishing & Maintaining Relationships
- Resolving Conflict, Negotiating With Others
- Coaching and Developing Others
- Interpreting Meaning of Information To Others
- Judging Qualities of Things, Services, People
- Performing for/Working with Public
- Staffing Organizational Units

These activities used in selecting jobs take full advantage of the Idealists' people orientation, mentoring skills, and ability to create harmony.

The next factors that went into determining the top jobs for Idealists were their interests, based on six well-defined interest areas. They are:

- *Realistic* - Are you interested in jobs that require athletic or mechanical ability, working with objects, machines, tools, plants or animals, or being outdoors?
- *Investigative* - Are you interested in jobs with people who like to observe, learn, investigate, analyze, evaluate or solve problems?
- *Artistic* - Are you interested in jobs involving artistic, innovative or intuitive abilities, and like to work in unstructured creative situations?

- *Social* - Do you like to work with people to inform, help, train, enlighten, develop or cure or are you skilled with words?
- *Enterprising* - Are you interested in jobs where you work with people to influence, perform, persuade, or lead for organizational goals or economic gain?
- *Conventional* - Are you interested in jobs that involve working with data, clerical tasks, or numerical ability, carrying things out in detail or following instructions?

Both the top interest areas and the order of their importance were used to filter good job matches for the Idealists.

Finally, a list of values appealing to Idealists was used to make sure that the jobs would match not only skills, activities, and interests, but key values. In fact, often the first thing you notice about another person is an expression of their values. For example, the top Idealist values are:

THE VALUES OF IDEALISTS
- Creativity
- Social Service
- Moral Values
- Working Conditions
- Co-workers
- Supervision, Human Relations
- Support

If you have taken the Keirsey Temperament Sorter, and if the skills, activities and values in the tables above appeal to your sense of a job, then you are probably on the right track reading about Idealists. You should continue on to the next chapter with descriptions of Idealist roles and actual jobs. If not, please explore the chapters on the other three temperaments to find your ideal career.

CHAPTER 9

THE IDEALIST ROLES

ACCORDING TO temperament theory, Idealists tend toward one of two roles: Mentor or Advocate, which differ enough from each other that there is a separate list of jobs for each.

MENTORS – THE TEACHES AND THE COUNSELORS

Mentors are the direction-oriented Idealists. They take on the roles of teaching and counseling, the benevolent and ethical ways of shaping the thoughts of others. They are *role directive*, which means that they are more apt to facilitate change in others, capturing the needs of the group or individual and developing their potential and actions. They are the people you picture when you think of a trusted advisor, someone in whose hands you place your finances, education, well-being, and life. Operators come in two role variants – Teachers and Counselors – both of which share the traits of directing and developing. Myers referred to the Teacher as the ENFJ and the Counselor as the INFJ.

Teachers tend to be more expressive, as you might imagine, able to grab the attention of an individual, but at their best in front of a group. They can motivate, educate, and facilitate with ease. Counselors are more reserved, preferring to work one-on-one with others. They do not motivate or educate so much as they advise and really drill down into the needs of the individuals they counsel.

When not satisfied in their current career, or when looking for a new career, Mentors seem to look for something to cure their disillusionment. Often in their career they are initially drawn to jobs they find intellectually stimulating and challenging. However, being perfectionists, they can become critical of the worth they actually bring to their position and others. For example, the following are typical Mentor reactions to job changes:

> I am really lost right now. I have been out of school for 5 years and I am working on my different 4th job. I am in the sales field and I really like it, but it seems like every time I get a job it doesn't turn out like I want it to. Like a good sales representative, I ask a lot of questions during the interviewing process, but the answers I get don't turn out to be as true as the interviewer paints the picture.

✖   ✖   ✖

I am a 39-year-old mom who is eager to return to the work force after spending 8 years at home raising my three children. In my former life I received an MBA in finance and worked in the investment management field as a bond trader/analyst. I found it less than fulfilling (although quite lucrative) and was happy to leave to be with my babies. Now, I am eager to rejoin the working world, but am adamant that a new job will be flexible enough to work around my children's schedules, yet also be intellectually challenging, useful to someone in some way, and part time. Finance writer, psychologist, and non-profit organization worker seem plausible and interesting occupations, but I am very anxious about making a mistake at my age.

JOBS FOR MENTORS

The jobs listed on the next pages are top matches for Mentors, but by no means the only careers you should consider. Listed next to each standard job classification are the total number of people employed in that occupation in the United States and the salary ranges. The "starting" salary is the number that 90% of people in that job earn more than. The "high" salary is the number that 90% of people in that job earn less than. So 80% of the people in a job earn between the starting and high salary figures. The "median" is the number that half the people earn more than and half earn less than. These are national averages, and you could earn more or less.

It Takes All Types

The jobs in bold are the "best of the best" for your temperament and role. These are based on the degree to which the job fit your personality and also the number of available jobs, relative to the amount of people of your temperament in the population. For example, Area, Ethnic, and Cultural Studies Teacher, Postsecondary would be a good job for a Mentor, but with only about 4,000 positions available nationwide, it would not be as helpful to list it as a top job. However, it helps to list it because the skill might be similar to another job you are considering, or it may point you in a direction that you would otherwise have missed.

Finally, the jobs are in rough order from the lowest skill level *for the skills required of the job* to the highest level. For example, Producer is a job listed early, and so would have a lower "level" than Director- Stage, Motion Pictures, Television, and Radio. Both jobs would seem roughly equivalent, yet Director has a higher level and is a top job (bold). This is because the top skills of the Mentor are more important to the Director job (as defined in the O*Net database) than to the Producer.

Best Fit Jobs for Mentors (Teachers and Counselors)

Job Title	Estimated Employment	Salary		
		Starting	Median	High
Legal Secretaries.	270,670	22,440	34,740	50,970
Forest Fire Fighting and Prevention Supervisors.	59,500	31,820	51,990	77,700

Producers.	46,750	21,050	41,030	87,770
Librarians.	139,460	25,030	41,700	62,990
Municipal Fire Fighting and Prevention Supervisors.	59,500	31,820	51,990	77,700
Counseling Psychologists.	**103,120**	**28,090**	**48,320**	**76,840**
Middle School Teachers, Except Special and Vocational Education.	**561,200**	**26,560**	**39,750**	**61,130**
Vocational Education Teachers, Middle School.	19,010	27,040	39,330	57,590
Secondary School Teachers, Except Special and Vocational Education.	**933,800**	**26,260**	**40,870**	**64,920**
Vocational Education Teachers, Secondary School.	**103,200**	**28,460**	**42,080**	**61,580**
Special Education Teachers, Middle School.	**87,790**	**26,500**	**38,600**	**61,590**

Special Education Teachers, Secondary School.	116,760	27,180	41,290	67,030
Elementary School Teachers, Except Special Education.	1,409,140	25,810	39,700	62,600
Dietitians and Nutritionists.	43,030	23,680	38,450	54,940
Fitness Trainers and Aerobics Instructors.	157,230	13,150	22,790	54,030
Art Directors.	20,560	30,130	56,880	109,440
Directors, Religious Activities and Education.	13,610	13,850	27,000	50,600
Commercial and Industrial Designers.	33,910	27,290	48,780	77,790
First–Line Supervisors, Administrative Support and Customer Service.	1,394,640	22,070	36,420	60,600
Residential Advisors.	42,630	13,710	20,060	32,660
Advertising and Promotions Managers.	93,420	27,840	53,360	119,310

The Idealist Roles

Sales Agents, Securities and Commodities.	269,310	24,770	56,080	*
Curators.	*(no data available)*		
Directors– Stage, Motion Pictures, Television, and Radio.	**46,750**	**21,050**	**41,030**	**87,770**
Chiropractors.	16,740	22,910	67,030	
Nursing Instructors and Teachers, Postsecondary.	35,870	29,200	47,650	71,430
Product Safety Engineers.	42,800	34,710	54,630	82,320
Adult Literacy, Remedial Education, and GED Teachers and Instructors.	53,250	19,700	33,540	59,280
Agents and Business Managers of Artists, Performers, and Athletes.	6,600	20,810	57,040	*
Registered Nurses.	**2,189,670**	**31,890**	**44,840**	**64,360**

Substance Abuse and Behavioral Disorder Counselors.	56,080	18,850	28,510	43,210
Mental Health Counselors.	65,780	18,500	27,570	46,270
Medical and Public Health Social Workers.	103,390	22,490	34,790	53,160
Mental Health and Substance Abuse Social Workers.	79,740	19,300	30,170	48,750
Audio–Visual Collections Specialists.	8,740	16,670	33,290	59,010
Audio and Video Equipment Technicians.	34,110	16,630	30,310	68,720
Physical Therapists.	120,410	38,510	54,810	83,370
Marketing Managers.	202,100	35,950	71,240	133,300
Landscape Architects.	17,130	26,300	43,540	74,100
Financial Managers, Branch or Department.	622,890	36,050	67,020	131,120

Psychiatric Technicians.	53,350	16,150	24,420	39,310
Optometrists.	23,880	40,450	82,860	*
Program Directors.	46,750	21,050	41,030	87,770
Educational Psychologists.	103,120	28,090	48,320	76,840
Child Support, Missing Persons, and Unemployment Insurance Fraud Investigators.	87,090	29,600	48,870	72,160
Property, Real Estate, and Community Association Managers.	145,340	16,720	36,020	80,360
Editors.	**104,210**	**22,460**	**39,370**	**73,330**
Educational, Vocational, and School Counselors.	**188,000**	**23,560**	**42,110**	**67,170**
Social and Community Service Managers.	93,460	23,450	39,130	67,920
Sales Managers.	344,180	34,700	68,520	137,780

Medical and Clinical Laboratory Technologists.	144,530	29,240	40,510	55,560
Financial Examiners.	23,560	30,090	53,060	100,130
Child, Family, and School Social Workers.	**266,570**	**20,120**	**31,470**	**50,280**
Human Resources Managers.	**224,970**	**33,360**	**59,000**	**104,020**
Compensation and Benefits Managers.			*(no data available)*	
Health Specialties Teachers, Postsecondary.	78,680	29,550	59,220	130,190
Computer Systems Analysts.	463,300	37,460	59,330	89,040
Engineering Managers.	242,280	52,350	84,070	130,350
Education Administrators, Elementary and Secondary School.	196,390	46,300	66,930	96,660
Education Administrators, Postsecondary.	**92,280**	**32,650**	**59,480**	**109,280**
Clinical Psychologists.	**103,120**	**28,090**	**48,320**	**76,840**

The Idealist Roles

Vocational Education Teachers Postsecondary.	**115,080**	**21,840**	**38,170**	**65,610**
Computer Software Engineers, Applications.	374,640	42,710	67,670	106,680
Computer Software Engineers, Systems Software.	264,610	43,600	69,530	105,240
Computer Programmers.	530,730	35,020	57,590	93,210
Anthropology and Archeology Teachers, Postsecondary.	4,400	30,110	56,540	88,890
Area, Ethnic, and Cultural Studies Teachers, Postsecondary.	4,070	30,780	52,290	91,440
Economics Teachers, Postsecondary.	11,530	32,920	61,180	100,920
Political Science Teachers, Postsecondary.	10,820	30,400	53,520	90,920

Psychology Teachers, Postsecondary.	24,000	27,230	51,640	89,770
Sociology Teachers, Postsecondary.	13,760	25,780	48,010	81,780
History Teachers, Postsecondary.	16,630	28,180	49,080	83,730
Clergy.	**30,980**	**15,350**	**31,760**	**54,550**
Government Service Executives.	**519,890**	**46,390**	**113,810**	*****
Psychiatrists.	21,280	50,930	118,640	*
Industrial– Organizational Psychologists.	1,280	36,410	66,880	110,460
Art, Drama, and Music Teachers, Postsecondary.	**55,160**	**23,120**	**45,530**	**81,710**
English Language and Literature Teachers, Postsecondary.	50,560	24,000	44,310	78,390
Foreign Language and Literature Teachers, Postsecondary.	18,380	25,680	44,380	77,660

Agricultural Sciences Teachers, Postsecondary.	10,720	31,860	62,690	93,860
Biological Science Teachers, Postsecondary.	36,910	29,770	54,450	109,660
Forestry and Conservation Science Teachers, Postsecondary.	1,980	36,360	58,110	92,790
Industrial Engineers.	171,810	38,140	58,580	86,370
Archivists.		*(no data available)*		
Public Relations Specialists.	**128,570**	**22,780**	**39,580**	**70,480**
Private Sector Executives.	519,890	46,390	113,810	*
Physician Assistants.	55,490	32,690	61,910	88,100
Occupational Therapists.	75,150	32,040	49,450	70,810
Respiratory Therapists.	82,670	28,620	37,680	50,660
Licensed Practical and Licensed Vocational Nurses.	679,470	21,520	29,440	41,800
Management Analysts.	**357,610**	**32,860**	**55,040**	**98,210**

Engineering Teachers, Postsecondary.	26,940	35,540	65,640	107,980
Mathematical Science Teachers, Postsecondary.	37,660	25,290	47,440	85,010
Computer Science Teachers, Postsecondary.	27,770	24,980	46,890	85,490
Agricultural Engineers.	2,170	33,660	55,850	91,600
Judges, Magistrate Judges, and Magistrates.	25,190	19,320	86,760	134,660
Family and General Practitioners.	**132,620**	**44,970**	**114,170**	*
Internists, General.	50,450	77,720	142,400	*
Obstetricians and Gynecologists.	18,240	98,490	*	*

*Indicates a salary greater than $145,000 per year.

Bold indicates this is a top job, based on both fit and/or total employment.

The jobs listed here are just the beginning. It is important to read through all the jobs for your temperament, and to browse the jobs for the other temperaments. This will ensure that you have identified your temperament correctly. Then, refer to chapter 12 for where to go from here.

ADVOCATES – THE CHAMPIONS AND THE HEALERS

Advocates are the *role informative* Idealists. Being *role informative*, they tend to be less directive than Mentors, giving information in return rather than direction. They are more apt to stand up for others, giving a voice to individuals and groups they feel lack one, with the hope of coming to a harmonious resolution or understanding. Advocates come in two role variants – Champions and Healers – both of which share the traits of directing and developing. Myers referred to the Champion as the ENFP and the Healer as the INFP.

Champions possess a lust for life, combined with a hunger for experience. They use these experiences to put together a big picture of the world both as it is and as they feel it should be, and they "champion" the ideals and values gained from these experiences. Healers are the more reserved Advocates. They tend to be focused more on championing the truth within the individual, creating a whole within the person. The picture of the world that Healers put together is expressed not by outward championing, but by internal reflection on healing divisions.

When not satisfied in their current career, or when looking for a new career, Advocates seem to have too many choices and possibilities. Being open to all types of experiences and willing to explore any path, they often seek to leave jobs that do not meet their needs for inspiration. However, they often must find focus and direction before they can complete – or even begin – a job search. For example, the following are typical Advocate reactions to job changes:

> Most of my jobs have been in event/conference planning which doesn't stimulate me at all, as it is primarily behind-the-scenes work, with too much paper shuffling, attending to details and organizing. I'm good at it, but I absolutely hate it. Usually I get overwhelmed easily by information overload and feel that I need to work so much harder than everyone else to manage everything. I've always been motivated by the number of opportunities that are out there and have used my creativity, energy and resourcefulness to further my pursuit of career happiness. My belief is that I need to get out there and find something that's going to move me because nobody else is going to bring it to me.

✂ ✂ ✂

> I am a creative person. I've been thinking about being an Art/Dance Therapist (MA), Film school, Writing (MA), Acupuncturist, ethno-botanist (MA in Anthropology). I've also thought about a travel tour manager/guide and travel writing. I just don't know if I can make a living doing these things and wonder if I shouldn't consider them because of job outlook for these fields. How do I know what the outlook is?

THE IDEALIST ROLES

JOBS FOR ADVOCATES

The jobs listed on the next pages are top matches for Advocates, but by no means the only careers you should consider. Listed next to each standard job classification are the total number of people employed in that occupation in the United States and the salary ranges. The "starting" salary is the number that 90% of people in that job earn more than. The "high" salary is the number that 90% of people in that job earn less than. So 80% of the people in a job earn between the starting and high salary figures. The "median" is the number that half the people earn more than and half earn less than. These are national averages, and you could earn more or less.

The jobs in bold are the "best of the best" for your temperament and role. These are based on the degree to which the job fit your personality and also the number of available jobs, relative to the amount of people of your temperament in the population. For example, Forestry and Conservation Science Teachers, Postsecondary would be a good job for an Advocate, but with only about 2,000 positions available nationwide, it would not be as helpful to list it as a top job. However, it helps to list it because the skill might be similar to another job you are considering, or it may point you in a direction that you would otherwise have missed.

Finally, the jobs are in rough order from the lowest skill level *for the skills required of the job* to the highest level. For example, Producer is a job listed early, and so would have a lower "level" than Director- Stage, Motion Pictures, Television, and Radio. Both jobs would seem roughly equivalent, yet Director has a higher level and is a top job (bold). This is because the top skills of the Advocate are more important to the Director job (as defined in the O*Net database) than to the Producer.

Best Fit Jobs for Advocates (Champions and Healers)

Job Title	Estimated Employment	Salary		
		Starting	Median	High
Set Designers.	8,470	13,820	31,440	57,400
Municipal Fire Fighters.	251,060	16,710	34,170	55,290
Forest Fire Fighting and Prevention Supervisors.	59,500	31,820	51,990	77,700
Producers.	46,750	21,050	41,030	87,770
Librarians.	139,460	25,030	41,700	62,990
Creative and Copy Writers.	41,410	20,290	42,270	81,370
Counseling Psychologists.	103,120	28,090	48,320	76,840
Middle School Teachers, Except Special and Vocational Education.	561,200	26,560	39,750	61,130

Vocational Education Teachers, Middle School.	19,010	27,040	39,330	57,590
Secondary School Teachers, Except Special and Vocational Education.	933,800	26,260	40,870	64,920
Vocational Education Teachers, Secondary School.	103,200	28,460	42,080	61,580
Special Education Teachers, Preschool, Kindergarten, and Elementary School.	208,970	26,640	40,880	66,210
Special Education Teachers, Middle School.	87,790	26,500	38,600	61,590
Special Education Teachers, Secondary School.	116,760	27,180	41,290	67,030
Elementary School Teachers, Except Special Education.	1,409,140	25,810	39,700	62,600

Dietitians and Nutritionists.	43,030	23,680	38,450	54,940
Fitness Trainers and Aerobics Instructors.	**157,230**	**13,150**	**22,790**	**54,030**
Art Directors.	20,560	30,130	56,880	109,440
Directors, Religious Activities and Education.	13,610	13,850	27,000	50,600
Commercial and Industrial Designers.	33,910	27,290	48,780	77,790
First–Line Supervisors, Administrative Support and Customer Service.	1,394,640	22,070	36,420	60,600
Residential Advisors.	42,630	13,710	20,060	32,660
Advertising and Promotions Managers.	**93,420**	**27,840**	**53,360**	**119,310**
Recreational Therapists.	26,940	17,010	28,650	43,810

Directors– Stage, Motion Pictures, Television, and Radio.	**46,750**	**21,050**	**41,030**	**87,770**
Chiropractors.	16,740	22,910	67,030	*
Nursing Instructors and Teachers, Postsecondary.	35,870	29,200	47,650	71,430
Adult Literacy, Remedial Education, and GED Teachers and Instructors.	53,250	19,700	33,540	59,280
Self–Enrichment Education Teachers.	**125,960**	**14,480**	**27,960**	**52,790**
Agents and Business Managers of Artists, Performers, and Athletes.	6,600	20,810	57,040	*
Registered Nurses.	**2,189,670**	**31,890**	**44,840**	**64,360**
Substance Abuse and Behavioral Disorder Counselors.	**56,080**	**18,850**	**28,510**	**43,210**

Mental Health Counselors.	**65,780**	**18,500**	**27,570**	**46,270**
Medical and Public Health Social Workers.	**103,390**	**22,490**	**34,790**	**53,160**
Mental Health and Substance Abuse Social Workers.	**79,740**	**19,300**	**30,170**	**48,750**
Poets and Lyricists.	**41,410**	**20,290**	**42,270**	**81,370**
Audio–Visual Collections Specialists.	8,740	16,670	33,290	59,010
Audio and Video Equipment Technicians.	34,110	16,630	30,310	68,720
Physical Therapists.	**120,410**	**38,510**	**54,810**	**83,370**
Marketing Managers.	**202,100**	**35,950**	**71,240**	**133,300**
Psychiatric Technicians.	53,350	16,150	24,420	39,310
Atmospheric and Space Scientists.	7,290	29,880	58,510	89,060
Optometrists.	23,880	40,450	82,860	*
Program Directors.	46,750	21,050	41,030	87,770

Educational Psychologists.	103,120	28,090	48,320	76,840
Property, Real Estate, and Community Association Managers.	145,340	16,720	36,020	80,360
Editors.	104,210	22,460	39,370	73,330
Educational, Vocational, and School Counselors.	188,000	23,560	42,110	67,170
Fashion Designers.	10,460	24,710	48,530	103,970
Social and Community Service Managers.	93,460	23,450	39,130	67,920
Health Educators.	43,670	20,150	33,860	57,430
Child, Family, and School Social Workers.	266,570	20,120	31,470	50,280
Podiatrists.	7,870	48,130	107,560	*
Human Resources Managers.	224,970	33,360	59,000	104,020
Health Specialties Teachers, Postsecondary.	78,680	29,550	59,220	130,190

Computer Systems Analysts.	463,300	37,460	59,330	89,040
Engineering Managers.	242,280	52,350	84,070	130,350
Education Administrators, Preschool and Child Care Center/Program.	49,460	18,270	30,420	65,030
Education Administrators, Elementary and Secondary School.	196,390	46,300	66,930	96,660
Actors.	63,500	12,700	25,920	93,620
Education Administrators, Postsecondary.	**92,280**	**32,650**	**59,480**	**109,280**
Clinical Psychologists.	**103,120**	**28,090**	**48,320**	**76,840**
Vocational Education Teachers Postsecondary.	**115,080**	**21,840**	**38,170**	**65,610**
Computer Software Engineers, Applications.	374,640	42,710	67,670	106,680

Computer Programmers.	**530,730**	**35,020**	**57,590**	**93,210**
Anthropology and Archeology Teachers, Postsecondary.	4,400	30,110	56,540	88,890
Area, Ethnic, and Cultural Studies Teachers, Postsecondary.	4,070	30,780	52,290	91,440
Political Science Teachers, Postsecondary.	10,820	30,400	53,520	90,920
Psychology Teachers, Postsecondary.	24,000	27,230	51,640	89,770
Sociology Teachers, Postsecondary.	13,760	25,780	48,010	81,780
History Teachers, Postsecondary.	16,630	28,180	49,080	83,730
Clergy.	30,980	15,350	31,760	54,550
Psychiatrists.	21,280	50,930	118,640	*
Industrial–Organizational Psychologists.	1,280	36,410	66,880	110,460

Art, Drama, and Music Teachers, Postsecondary.	**55,160**	**23,120**	**45,530**	**81,710**
English Language and Literature Teachers, Postsecondary.	50,560	24,000	44,310	78,390
Foreign Language and Literature Teachers, Postsecondary.	18,380	25,680	44,380	77,660
Agricultural Sciences Teachers, Postsecondary.	10,720	31,860	62,690	93,860
Biological Science Teachers, Postsecondary.	36,910	29,770	54,450	109,660
Forestry and Conservation Science Teachers, Postsecondary.	1,980	36,360	58,110	92,790
Home Health Aides.	561,120	12,770	17,120	24,810
Archivists.	*(no data available)*			
Public Relations Specialists.	**128,570**	**22,780**	**39,580**	**70,480**
Private Sector Executives.	519,890	46,390	113,810	*
Physician Assistants.	55,490	32,690	61,910	88,100

Occupational Therapists.	75,150	32,040	49,450	70,810
Respiratory Therapists.	82,670	28,620	37,680	50,660
Licensed Practical and Licensed Vocational Nurses.	679,470	21,520	29,440	41,800
Broadcast News Analysts.			*(no data available)*	
Management Analysts.	**357,610**	**32,860**	**55,040**	**98,210**
Emergency Medical Technicians and Paramedics.	165,530	14,660	22,460	37,760
Family and General Practitioners.	**132,620**	**44,970**	**114,170**	*
Internists, General.	50,450	77,720	142,400	*
Obstetricians and Gynecologists.	18,240	98,490	*	*
Pediatricians, General.	25,580	77,980	125,970	*

*Indicates a salary greater than $145,000 per year.

Bold indicates this is a top job, based on both fit and/or total employment.

It Takes All Types

The jobs listed here are just the beginning. It is important to read through all the jobs for your temperament, and to browse the jobs for the other temperaments. This will ensure that you have identified your temperament correctly. Then, refer to chapter 12 for where to go from here.

CHAPTER 10

RATIONALS

MADELINE WAS ALWAYS GOOD at science and math. Even though she felt like "science was for boys" those were the subjects that interested her most in high school. When she applied to college, she really didn't know what she wanted to do with her education and career, other than she liked science and math and was good at them. She literally picked her college major – food science – off a list of majors in science because "It was an applied science." Madeline wanted to do something that had some relevance, and so did not go into theoretical science or math. After graduating, she went to work for a division of Schilling as a "technician," in food science, and was promoted to "scientist."

It Takes All Types

Madeline left to go to Del Monte, the place she has spent the bulk of her career. She started there working on brand maintenance and transitioned into managing new products as her skills and abilities were quickly recognized. She uses her knowledge of chemistry and biology to study the processing of foods and to research and determine the best ways to process, package, preserve, store, and distribute food. Madeline was recently out of work for a year when she quit after most of her staff was laid off. During that time she pursued some of her hobbies, such as music (playing in the community concert band), pottery, and cooking. Even though Madeline is a food scientist, when she cooks at home she uses the recipe she is preparing mainly as inspiration, with lots of substituting of ingredients and improvising technique. In the workplace Madeline says her supervisors both value her competence and like her. However, as a manager she feels that she sometimes intimidates her subordinates. When I asked her why this was, she thought it was due to her high standards, which she expects herself and her staff to uphold. She was quick to add that she feels she is fair and listens to the needs of her staff well.

Madeline views her strength as being a good manager – a proactive project leader who plans ahead and has "contingency plans" if necessary. She said she sometimes lacks follow-through on projects and also noted a tendency to procrastinate on things she does not enjoy. Looking back on her career, Madeline felt she was not as "political" as she should have been, relating better to her peers whom she feels are competent and understand the work she and they are doing, rather than to supervisors who may not have a grasp of the real work. Overall, Madeline has enjoyed her career and utilizing her skills to research, analyze, and create some of the products we all enjoy on a daily basis. Madeline is an ideal illustration of the Rational temperament.

Rationals comprise less than 10% of the United States population. They may be scarce, but a little goes a long way. If the Guardian's role is to belong to society and create its order, the Artisan's role to be unrestrained and adaptable as troubleshooters and artists, and Idealist's role to nurture harmonious relationships and personal development, then it is the Rational's role to understand and control everything around them. The Rational must understand the systems they come into contact with – social, economic, biological, physical, and solar (including the universe beyond). This drive for knowledge, competence, and achievement results in giving the Rational what they desire: power. That is, comprehensive power, explanatory power, predictive power, and the power to control.

Rationals are rarely seen in most workplaces, not only because their numbers are few, but also because they tend to congregate in careers with other Rationals. Still, when you do run across them, they stand out vividly for their demeanor, which includes terse, formal speech with an absence of "small talk," deliberate actions, self-reliance, and often a sense of aloofness or arrogance. They are the people often referred to as "aliens," "geeks," and "Spock" (the half-human, half-Vulcan character from Star Trek who based all decisions on pure logic and reason). Their work areas can be either messy or neat, and often this depends on whether they are in the middle of a project (or several projects) at the moment. Even if piles of paper or equipment are strewn about, the Rational surely knows where to get what he or she needs from the "disorder."

The occupations that allow the Rational the ability to carry out research and gain knowledge can be quite varied. This depends upon whether the Rational has a need to see their knowledge, competency, ability and ingenuity directly translated into action (a product or service), like Madeline (a Rational Mastermind), or whether they are comfortable to take on the primarily more theoretical work that precedes the practical applicability. If the Rational does seek to see the final product, they are often drawn to applied sciences in economics, medicine, and biology or to management positions in government, education, or business. On the other hand, if the Rational is less *directive*, and more *informative*, they can be found in the theoretical sciences, architecture, consulting, forensic science, and as post-secondary professors of science, math, or language.

Keirsey tells us that the Rationals are abstract in the use of words. You can use this to spot Rationals in conversation, where they will talk primarily about the future – the great abstraction in which they spend much of their time – in terms of the theories they are currently working on, what they hope to find, and perhaps how they can translate this into a product, with detailed strategy for every step in the process. But in contrast to Idealists, who have a fluency for both language and interpersonal communication, Rationals will have usually have to be coaxed to share their theories with all but those closest to them. They tend to be understated, calm, and "rational" in their explanations, but can become very excited by a new idea that has captured their imagination.

Rationals display the strategic intelligence. Strategy is devising or employing a plan or method to attain a defined goal. In contrast to tactics and the tactical intelligence, which is the domain of Artisans, strategy is not deployed immediately for short-term position or gain. Strategy is concerned with a goal in the future, which is the orientation of the abstract Rationals, and not the here-and-now of tactical Artisans. The long-term goals of Rationals revolve around increasing efficiency of the systems they study and ultimately seek control over. They seek to solve the problems that will allow for this increased efficiency because efficiency is their definition of perfection in a system. It is this perfection Rationals seek to discover and obtain.

Rationals are also utilitarian in their tool use. Like Artisans, Rational tool use is governed by the tool's usefulness rather than whether it is legal (as for Guardians) or moral (as for Idealists). In the broader sense of the word, almost everything physical around us is a tool: our homes are tools for protection from the elements, cars are tools for moving ourselves, streets tools for carrying cars, and so on. The Rational might say "Here is a car, what is the speed at which it will achieve the greatest fuel economy?", without concern for the legal speed limit or the morality of using those resources. In fact, if there were a more efficient alternative, the Rational would embrace that alternative, as long as it was pragmatic.

In the workforce, Rationals often have less trouble than might be expected given the alienation they often experience growing up and during adolescence. In fact, it is often not until their more advanced college courses and graduate school that Rationals really shine, finally finding application for their strategic intellect, theories that capture their imagination, and understanding from peers. The places Rationals usually find this support is in research programs in universities, government service, and the R&D departments of corporations, particularly technology and medical companies. However, in more traditional companies or settings, with a more normal distribution of temperaments, Rationals can experience some of the same difficulties they encountered early in life. They can present as snobbish or arrogant, cold and uncaring, and independent and unwilling to be a team player. It takes study and control for this Rational to learn to play along with roles around them, which they can do if they are interested in staying in that setting.

THE SELF-IMAGE OF RATIONALS

It is important to understand what makes up the self-image of ourselves and others if we are going to be able to effectively communicate, lead, follow, motivate, and appreciate each other in the workplace. Our self-image, according to Keirsey, is composed of three main attributes: self-esteem, self-respect, and self-confidence.

Self-esteem for Rationals is tied to their ingenuity. Whatever the job they are doing, the Rational must bring an ingenious creativity to it. Put another way, the job must be so challenging that only the Rational's inventiveness can solve it. Otherwise, why would the Rational do it? Better to let someone else take care of more routine matters. Rationals apply this ingenuity in other aspects of their life, such as their recreation or hobbies, where they use their ingenuity to acquire new skills and perfect those they already have. Others would view this kind of "play" as "work," but to the Rational they are not separate, and hobbies are really other expertise that Rationals posses, though usually (but not always) unpaid.

For Rationals, self-respect comes from independence. Rationals cannot bear the thought of relying on someone or something else *beyond their control* for any part of their direction, thought, or action. They will accept rules, regulations, and laws, but only after they have considered their usefulness from a logical point of view, and not simply because they exist. This autonomy Rationals display can also cause distress in the workplace, where a person's title or rank means little or nothing to them, preferring to judge the person based on their ideas and contributions.

Self-confidence for Rationals arises from their determination. If a Rational cannot trust in his or her own will power, they feel they may fail at their objective. To make a proclamation to himself to reach a goal creates self-confidence in the Rational, since upon imagining the goal he begins to strategize ways to reach that goal, and it becomes more and more real. The feeling of having reached a strategic goal is a good and empowering feeling. The Rational's determination must at that point become strong to carry that vision of reality into that which is real. Without that determination, the goal will likely not be reached, and the Rational's self-confidence will be undermined.

ARCHETYPE AND CARICATURE

Albert Einstein has been hailed as the quintessential Rational. Einstein constantly hungered for knowledge of the laws of physics and the workings of the universe. Einstein developed the special and general theories of relativity and contributed to other areas of physics, including thermodynamics and quantum physics. For the most part, Einstein played an informative role as a professor and theoretician, always acquiring knowledge and producing new ideas for how the natural world works, leaving others to develop useful inventions – products or processes – from his work.

If Albert Einstein is the Rational archetype, then Dr. Strangelove is the Rational caricature. In the movie *Dr. Strangelove*, the doctor is an ex-Nazi scientist working for the United States military. There is a crises when a Russian-made "doomsday device" is about to be unleashed. Dr. Strangelove tells the President, "I would not rule out the chance to preserve a nucleus of human specimens," and continues, laying out a plan for the species to survive underground at the bottom of some deep mine shafts.

Dr. Strangelove continues describing the computer program he would create to decide who would be saved and who would be left behind for the 100-year duration. "Of course, it would be absolutely vital that our top government and military men be included…to foster the principles of leadership and tradition." He goes on to explain his breeding program, with a ratio of ten females to each male, so they could "work their way back to the present Gross national Product in twenty years." The Rational's strategic intellect, with long-range plans and contingencies for any event, is evident, if extreme.

Another example comes from the HBO series *Sex and the City*. The show revolves around the lives of four women living in New York – each of whom seems to embody a different temperament. Miranda is a partner in a corporate law firm, and she is portrayed as opinionated, decisive, organized, overachieving, and analytical. She is usually the one to offer the pragmatic advice and stick to it. In dating, she shows the typical Rational reluctance to "play" and does not like making relationship small talk. In one scene, sick of hearing about the other three women's dating problems, she says, "Can we change the subject?", then reaches into her purse, and shouts, "Hey! Look at my new palm Pilot." Rationals tend to love gadgets.

MANAGING, LEADING, AND ENTREPRENEURSHIP

Rationals bring vision to an organization. Their long-term, strategic vision starts with the principles upon which the organization is founded and builds up into a stable, efficient, and productive system for the future. Along the way, every assumption is questioned and tested to make sure it is the correct solution – the most efficient, taking into account the current and future needs of the entire organization. They excel at putting the personnel and the technology of the organization to good use. New ideas and technologies are embraced readily if they can be made to work for the organization, or discarded without prejudice if they cannot.

As entrepreneurs, Rationals display these same positive traits. They can turn a vision of a goal into a reality by creating an efficient organization through a grasp of both the big picture and the details overlaid with determination. Unlike the Artisan tactician who is concerned with making the most of today's efforts and interactions, seeking the better position and the winning of the battle, the Rational strategist is focused keenly on the future, building efficiencies and plans that will assure the war's victory. They may ignore or give less credence to the battles along the way, convinced that the war will be won. However, this can cause consternation among the rank and file, who may not be fully aware of the Rational's long-range plan. In fact, the Rational may appear cold and uncaring to his colleagues and subordinates, being so focused on the future and the goal. But in the end, it is often the Rational entrepreneur that creates the future by developing value and efficiency for their organization and the customers it serves.

Skills, Activities, Interests, and Values

In looking at career and job choices for the Rationals, we must consider the skills, activities, interests, and values of the person and the job. While your skills and interests may be different from other Rationals, the jobs presented have been shown to be those that interest a large portion of Rationals and that display skills that build naturally on the strategic intelligence. There is a range of activities and skill levels in the jobs presented in the next chapter, and the list is by no means exhaustive. It is meant to both illustrate the principles of finding a job that fits your temperament well and to point you in a series of directions for the skill level you have acquired or are willing to acquire.

Rationals' skills are developed through use and practice of the strategic intellect. These skills, in the job language of the Occupational Information Network (O*Net) sponsored by the U.S. Department of Labor, are presented in the following table.

THE SKILLS OF RATIONALS
- Science
- Active Learning
- Critical Thinking
- Mathematics
- Systems Evaluation
- Idea Generation
- Programming
- Operations Analysis
- Identifying Downstream Consequences
- Technology Design
- Learning Strategies
- Solution Appraisal
- Systems Perception
- Synthesis/Reorganization

These are the skills that were primarily used in assessing the skill component of the Rational jobs. It is not necessarily that all of you display great aptitude in all these skills, but only that you recognize the ability to attain these skills through use will come more naturally to you. The jobs and careers presented in the next chapter will require some or all of these, and you can fill the bill by using your strategic intelligence.

There are 42 activities and over 100,000 activity entries for the 1100 jobs in the O*Net catalog. The top activities involved in the Rational jobs are the following:

THE ACTIVITIES OF RATIONALS

- Interacting With Computers
- Evaluating Info. Against Standards
- Getting Information Needed to Do the Job
- Processing Information
- Making Decisions and Solving Problems
- Judging Qualities of Things, Services, People
- Interpreting Meaning of Info. To Others
- Analyzing Data or Information
- Drafting & Specifying Tech. Devices, etc.
- Coordinating Work & Activities of Others

These activities used in selecting jobs take full advantage of the Rationals' data gathering, processing, interpreting, and coordinating orientation.

RATIONALS

The next factors that went into determining the top jobs for Rationals were their interests, based on six well-defined interest areas. They are:

- *Realistic* - Are you interested in jobs that require athletic or mechanical ability, working with objects, machines, tools, plants or animals, or being outdoors?
- *Investigative* - Are you interested in jobs with people who like to observe, learn, investigate, analyze, evaluate or solve problems?
- *Artistic* - Are you interested in jobs involving artistic, innovative or intuitive abilities, and like to work in unstructured creative situations?
- *Social* - Do you like to work with people to inform, help, train, enlighten, develop or cure or are you skilled with words?
- *Enterprising* - Are you interested in jobs where you work with people to influence, perform, persuade, or lead for organizational goals or economic gain?
- *Conventional* - Are you interested in jobs that involve working with data, clerical tasks, or numerical ability, carrying things out in detail or following instructions?

Both the top interest areas and the order of their importance were used to filter good job matches for the Rationals.

Finally, a list of values appealing to Rationals was used to make sure that the jobs would match not only skills, activities, and interests, but key values. In fact, often the first thing you notice about another person is an expression of their values. For example, the top Rational values are:

The Values of Rationals
- Independence
- Achievement
- Autonomy
- Supervision, Technical
- Responsibility
- Ability Utilization

If you have taken the Keirsey Temperament Sorter, and if the skills, activities and values in the tables above appeal to your sense of a job, then you are probably on the right track reading about Rationals. You should continue on to the next chapter with descriptions of Rational roles and actual jobs. If not, please explore the chapters on the other three temperaments to find your ideal career.

Chapter 11

The Rational Roles

According to temperament theory, Rationals tend toward one of two roles: Coordinator or Engineer, which differ enough from each other that there is a separate list of jobs for each.

Coordinators – the Fieldmarshals and the Masterminds

Coordinators are the direction-oriented Rationals. They take on the roles of mobilizing and entailing, giving direction both when and where it is needed. Being *role directive*, decisions come naturally to Coordinators, and if posed a question or problem, they will have a plan of action ready, with alternatives just in case, in short order. They are the ones who arrange – from people and organizations to operations and finances. Coordinators come in two role variants – Fieldmarshals and Masterminds – both of which share the traits of directing and coordinating. Myers referred to the Fieldmarshal as the ENTJ and the Mastermind as the INTJ.

Fieldmarshals tend to be more expressive, although quite directive, to the point of being terse. They forcibly grab the attention of an individual, but also possess a captivating charm. They can motivate, direct, and coordinate with ease. Masterminds are more reserved, preferring to work alone. They do not coordinate by direction, but rather by sequencing, or ordering. They will propose a plan of action based on the circumstances, ready to change the plan to accommodate new developments, either in circumstances or strategic directive.

When not satisfied in their current career, or when looking for a new career, Coordinators seem to consider a lot of possibilities, often in a hobby area. Possessing the confidence to tackle the job, and often the ability to succeed if given a chance, they lack only the knowledge or network for getting into a new field. They are impatient to start a new path at the bottom, feeling that their skills and ability should place them higher up the ladder. For example, the following are typical Coordinator reactions to job changes:

> I have no formal education but have been an office manager for over 12 years and am interested in a career move upward. For the last 6 years I've been employed as a manager of large housing complexes. Before that I was a comptroller at an industrial painting contractor. Am I a

chambermaid seeking Queen position or Queen stuck as a chambermaid?

❆　❆　❆

I have been trying to find my ideal job. I have been doing some exercises and have found my 3 favorite interests are Cooking, Fashion and Investing in the Stock Market. I have no idea how to find a field that will allow me to combine these interests. My professional experience has been in technology as a systems engineer. Unfortunately, I don't like doing this work at all and I don't want to do it anymore. Do you have any idea of areas that will allow me to combine my interests or how I can find information on how I can blend these interests into a career?

Jobs for Coordinators

The jobs listed on the next pages are top matches for Coordinators, but by no means the only careers you should consider. Listed next to each standard job classification are the total number of people employed in that occupation in the United States and the salary ranges. The "starting" salary is the number that 90% of people in that job earn more than. The "high" salary is the number that 90% of people in that job earn less than. So 80% of the people in a job earn between the starting and high salary figures. The "median" is the number that half the people earn more than and half earn less than. These are national averages, and you could earn more or less.

The jobs in bold are the "best of the best" for your temperament and role. These are based on the degree to which the job fit your personality and also the number of available jobs, relative to the amount of people of your temperament in the population. For example, Sociologist would be a good job for a Coordinator, but with only about 1,300 positions available nationwide, it would not be as helpful to list it as a top job. However, it helps to list it because the skill might be similar to another job you are considering, or it may point you in a direction that you would otherwise have missed.

Finally, the jobs are in rough order from the lowest skill level *for the skills required of the job* to the highest level. For example, Caption and Copy Writer is a job listed early, and so would have a lower "level" than Editor. Both jobs would seem roughly equivalent, yet Editor has a higher level and is a top job (bold). This is because the top skills of the Coordinator are more important to the Editor job (as defined in the O*Net database) than to the Caption and Copy Writer.

Best Fit Jobs for Coordinators (Fieldmarshals and Masterminds)

Job Title	Estimated	Salary		
	Employment	Starting	Median	High
Caption and Copy Writers.	41,410	20,290	42,270	81,370

Farm and Home Management Advisors.	10,290	17,940	36,290	61,580
Editors.	**104,210**	**22,460**	**39,370**	**73,330**
Technical Directors/Managers.	46,750	21,050	41,030	87,770
First–Line Supervisors/Managers of Food Preparation and Serving Workers.	624,180	14,870	22,680	37,740
Food Service Managers.	282,290	19,200	31,720	53,090
Fire Investigators.	11,900	24,790	41,630	65,030
Human Resources Managers.	224,970	33,360	59,000	104,020
Compensation and Benefits Managers.			*(no data available)*	
Computer Security Specialists.	234,040	32,450	51,280	81,150
Private Detectives and Investigators.	**28,700**	**16,210**	**26,750**	**52,200**
Forest Fire Fighting and Prevention Supervisors.	59,500	31,820	51,990	77,700
Program Directors.	46,750	21,050	41,030	87,770
Secondary School Teachers, Except Special and Vocational Education.	933,800	26,260	40,870	64,920

Vocational Education Teachers, Secondary School.	103,200	28,460	42,080	61,580
First–Line Supervisors and Manager/Supervisors– Construction Trades Workers.	502,010	28,660	44,790	70,780
Sales Agents, Securities and Commodities.	269,310	24,770	56,080	*
Radiologic Technologists.	172,080	25,310	36,000	52,050
First–Line Supervisors/Managers of Mechanics, Installers, and Repairers.	421,740	26,860	44,250	70,090
Police Detectives.	**87,090**	**29,600**	**48,870**	**72,160**
Biochemists.	13,440	32,310	54,230	93,330
Lodging Managers.	31,890	19,080	30,770	55,050
Counseling Psychologists.	**103,120**	**28,090**	**48,320**	**76,840**
Construction Managers.	229,200	34,820	58,250	102,860
Network Systems and Data Communications Analysts.	119,220	33,360	54,510	88,620
Producers.	46,750	21,050	41,030	87,770

Financial Managers, Branch or Department.	622,890	36,050	67,020	131,120
Audio–Visual Collections Specialists.	8,740	16,670	33,290	59,010
Audio and Video Equipment Technicians.	34,110	16,630	30,310	68,720
Advertising and Promotions Managers.	93,420	27,840	53,360	119,310
Clinical Psychologists.	103,120	28,090	48,320	76,840
Range Managers.	12,980	30,240	47,140	68,300
Database Administrators.	108,000	29,400	51,990	89,320
Economists.	**13,680**	**35,690**	**64,830**	**114,580**
Zoologists and Wildlife Biologists.	11,710	27,140	43,980	68,190
Directors– Stage, Motion Pictures, Television, and Radio.	46,750	21,050	41,030	87,770
Medical and Clinical Laboratory Technologists.	144,530	29,240	40,510	55,560
Materials Engineers.	24,430	37,680	59,100	87,630
Physician Assistants.	55,490	32,690	61,910	88,100
Pharmacists.	212,660	51,570	70,950	89,010
Soil Conservationists.	12,980	30,240	47,140	68,300
Public Relations Specialists.	128,570	22,780	39,580	70,480

Forest Fire Inspectors and Prevention Specialists.	1,040	17,060	32,140	50,680
Educational, Vocational, and School Counselors.	188,000	23,560	42,110	67,170
Computer and Information Systems Managers.	283,480	44,090	78,830	127,460
Statistical Assistants.	**22,050**	**17,390**	**27,870**	**43,060**
Computer Software Engineers, Applications.	374,640	42,710	67,670	106,680
Computer Software Engineers, Systems Software.	264,610	43,600	69,530	105,240
Computer Hardware Engineers.	63,680	42,620	67,300	107,360
Creative Writers.	41,410	20,290	42,270	81,370
Agricultural Crop Farm Managers.	5,370	20,940	38,400	75,420
Anthropology and Archeology Teachers, Postsecondary.	4,400	30,110	56,540	88,890
Economics Teachers, Postsecondary.	11,530	32,920	61,180	100,920
Political Science Teachers, Postsecondary.	10,820	30,400	53,520	90,920
Psychology Teachers, Postsecondary.	24,000	27,230	51,640	89,770

Sociology Teachers, Postsecondary.	13,760	25,780	48,010	81,780
Commercial and Industrial Designers.	33,910	27,290	48,780	77,790
Nuclear Medicine Technologists.	18,030	31,910	44,130	58,500
Commercial Pilots.	**18,040**	**24,290**	**43,300**	**92,000**
Anthropologists.	4,140	21,880	36,040	62,430
Administrative Law Judges, Adjudicators, and Hearing Officers.	12,560	32,970	61,240	111,590
Arbitrators, Mediators, and Conciliators.	4,850	23,360	43,060	93,170
Government Service Executives.	519,890	46,390	113,810	*
First–Line Supervisors/Managers of Police and Detectives.	113,740	34,660	57,210	86,060
Marketing Managers.	202,100	35,950	71,240	133,300
Education Administrators, Postsecondary.	92,280	32,650	59,480	109,280
Computer Programmers.	530,730	35,020	57,590	93,210
Management Analysts.	357,610	32,860	55,040	98,210
Environmental Scientists and Specialists, Including Health.	**54,860**	**28,520**	**44,180**	**73,790**

Medical Scientists, Except Epidemiologists.	**35,570**	**31,440**	**57,810**	**112,000**
Microbiologists.	15,880	30,420	48,890	84,790
Foresters.	9,890	27,330	43,640	65,960
Actuaries.	12,890	37,130	66,590	127,360
Archivists.			*(no data available)*	
Education Administrators, Elementary and Secondary School.	196,390	46,300	66,930	96,660
Biologists.			***(no data available)***	
Sociologists.	1,360	19,420	45,670	85,350
Private Sector Executives.	519,890	46,390	113,810	*
Hydrologists.	7,240	35,910	55,410	85,260
Geologists.	21,810	33,910	56,230	106,040
Mathematicians.	3,140	35,390	68,640	101,900
Chemists.	**82,320**	**29,620**	**50,080**	**88,030**
Materials Scientists.	8,660	33,120	60,620	99,820
Educational Psychologists.	103,120	28,090	48,320	76,840
Judges, Magistrate Judges, and Magistrates.	**25,190**	**19,320**	**86,760**	**134,660**
Technical Writers	**50,700**	**28,890**	**47,790**	**74,360**
Financial Analysts.	**159,490**	**31,880**	**52,420**	**101,760**
Plant Scientists.			*(no data available)*	
Astronomers.	910	38,310	74,510	112,550
Psychiatrists.	21,280	50,930	118,640	*

Engineering Managers.	242,280	52,350	84,070	130,350
Computer Systems Analysts.	463,300	37,460	59,330	89,040
Food Scientists and Technologists.				*(no data available)*
Natural Sciences Managers.	38,870	43,110	75,880	128,090
Lawyers.	**489,530**	**44,590**	**88,280**	*
Statisticians.	**17,520**	**28,430**	**51,990**	**86,660**
Agricultural Engineers.	2,170	33,660	55,850	91,600
Nuclear Engineers.	12,610	58,030	79,360	105,930
Physicists.	**8,990**	**51,680**	**83,310**	**116,290**
Urban and Regional Planners.	**28,850**	**29,890**	**46,500**	**72,090**

*Indicates a salary greater than $145,000 per year.

Bold indicates this is a top job, based on both fit and/or total employment.

The jobs listed here are just the beginning. It is important to read through all the jobs for your temperament, and to browse the jobs for the other temperaments. This will ensure that you have identified your temperament correctly. Then, refer to chapter 12 for where to go from here.

�֍   ✖   ✖

It Takes All Types

Engineers are the open-ended Rationals. They take on the roles of devising and designing, following the logic of their thoughts and ideas fully to their conclusions. Being *role informative*, ideas rather than directions are the playground of Engineers, and if posed a question or problem, they create and present a structure to address it, but will not likely be the ones to implement it. Engineers come in two role variants – Inventors and Architects – both of whom focus on the manner and intent of processes. Myers referred to the Inventor as the ENTP and the Architect as the INTP.

Inventors tend to be more expressive, developing the first versions of their inventions as a demonstration of their ideas. They create the prototypes upon which the many useful devices they create are built. These devices can be physical inventions, or legal, financial, or urban constructs waiting to be implemented. Architects are typically much more reserved, preferring to work alone. They are less apt to build prototypes, as they tend to build models of physical devices or structures on paper, ever perfecting the theoretical construct. The actual transformation into either prototype or working version is not important to them.

When not satisfied in their current career, or when looking for a new career, Engineers, like the Coordinators, seem to consider a lot of possibilities, often in another area they have pursued as a hobby. Unlike the Coordinators, they are not so impatient as to start small, and seem to enjoy learning new skills and taking on new academic programs. Still, they often need a push in one direction to get them motivated. For example, the following are typical Engineer reactions to job changes:

> For the past six years I have worked in the information technology field as an analyst. I found the work relatively enjoyable, but hated the corporate politics. I decided to take a break from working and figure out what I really want to be when I grow up. I want to do something that satisfies my creative bent. I have written a couple of children's stories and trying to see if I can get them published. I don't mind starting over at the bottom, but I can't get anyone to take me seriously. They just look at the past six years (and my income), and that's the end of it.

✂ ✂ ✂

> I'm willing and able to retrain but don't know where to go from here. I like solving problems but am easily bored with routine tasks. I'd like to do something that will allow me to use my creative side more (with ideas more than any innate artistic ability). I can't wait to earn another degree before landing a job, but what else can I do with a B.S. in Computer Science?

✂ ✂ ✂

It Takes All Types

Jobs for Engineers

The jobs listed on the next pages are top matches for
Engineers, but by no means the only careers you should consider.
Listed next to each standard job classification are the total number
of people employed in that occupation in the United States and the
salary ranges. The "starting" salary is the number that 90% of
people in that job earn more than. The "high" salary is the number
that 90% of people in that job earn less than. So 80% of the people
in a job earn between the starting and high salary figures. The
"median" is the number that half the people earn more than and
half earn less than. These are national averages, and you could
earn more or less.

The jobs in bold are the "best of the best" for your
temperament and role. These are based on the degree to which the
job fit your personality and also the number of available jobs,
relative to the amount of people of your temperament in the
population. For example, Astronomer would be a good job for an
Engineer, but with less than 1000 positions available nationwide, it
would not be as helpful to list it as a top job. However, it helps to
list it because the skill might be similar to another job you are
considering, or it may point you in a direction that you would
otherwise have missed.

Finally, the jobs are in rough order from the lowest skill level
for the skills required of the job to the highest level. For example,
Biochemist is a job listed early, and so would have a lower "level"
than Biophysicist. Both jobs would seem roughly equivalent, yet

Biophysicist has a higher level and is a top job (bold). This is because the top skills of the Engineer are more important to the Biophysicist job (as defined in the O*Net database) than to the Biochemist.

Best Fit Jobs for Engineers (Inventors and Architects)

Job Title	Estimated	Salary		
	Employment	Starting	Median	High
Editors.	**104,210**	**22,460**	**39,370**	**73,330**
Technical Directors/Managers.	46,750	21,050	41,030	87,770
Interpreters and Translators.	16,780	18,110	31,110	52,910
Fire Investigators.	11,900	24,790	41,630	65,030
Computer Security Specialists.	234,040	32,450	51,280	81,150
Private Detectives and Investigators.	**28,700**	**16,210**	**26,750**	**52,200**
Program Directors.	46,750	21,050	41,030	87,770
Secondary School Teachers, Except Special and Vocational Education.	933,800	26,260	40,870	64,920
Vocational Education Teachers, Secondary School.	103,200	28,460	42,080	61,580

Radiologic Technologists.	172,080	25,310	36,000	52,050
Police Detectives.	**87,090**	**29,600**	**48,870**	**72,160**
Biochemists.	13,440	32,310	54,230	93,330
Respiratory Therapists.	82,670	28,620	37,680	50,660
Counseling Psychologists.	103,120	28,090	48,320	76,840
Substance Abuse and Behavioral Disorder Counselors.	56,080	18,850	28,510	43,210
Mental Health Counselors.	65,780	18,500	27,570	46,270
Poets and Lyricists.	41,410	20,290	42,270	81,370
Network Systems and Data Communications Analysts.	119,220	33,360	54,510	88,620
Producers.	46,750	21,050	41,030	87,770
Atmospheric and Space Scientists.	7,290	29,880	58,510	89,060
Landscape Architects.	17,130	26,300	43,540	74,100
Audio and Video Equipment Technicians.	34,110	16,630	30,310	68,720
Clinical Psychologists.	103,120	28,090	48,320	76,840
Database Administrators.	108,000	29,400	51,990	89,320

Cartographers and Photogrammetrists.	7,360	23,560	39,410 64,780
Economists.	13,680	35,690	64,830 114,580
Biophysicists.	13,440	32,310	54,230 93,330
Zoologists and Wildlife Biologists.	11,710	27,140	43,980 68,190
Set Designers.	8,470	13,820	31,440 57,400
Directors– Stage, Motion Pictures, Television, and Radio.	46,750	21,050	41,030 87,770
Medical and Clinical Laboratory Technologists.	144,530	29,240	40,510 55,560
Materials Engineers.	24,430	37,680	59,100 87,630
Pharmacists.	212,660	51,570	70,950 89,010
Soil Conservationists.	12,980	30,240	47,140 68,300
Forest Fire Inspectors and Prevention Specialists.	1,040	17,060	32,140 50,680
Art Directors.	20,560	30,130	56,880 109,440
Computer and Information Systems Managers.	283,480	44,090	78,830 127,460
Statistical Assistants.	22,050	17,390	27,870 43,060
Orthodontists.			*(no data available)*
Chiropractors.	16,740	22,910	67,030 *

Computer Software Engineers, Applications.	374,640	42,710	67,670 106,680
Computer Software Engineers, Systems Software.	264,610	43,600	69,530 105,240
Computer Hardware Engineers.	63,680	42,620	67,300 107,360
Creative Writers.	41,410	20,290	42,270 81,370
Agricultural Crop Farm Managers.	5,370	20,940	38,400 75,420
Anthropology and Archeology Teachers, Postsecondary.	4,400	30,110	56,540 88,890
Economics Teachers, Postsecondary.	11,530	32,920	61,180 100,920
Political Science Teachers, Postsecondary.	10,820	30,400	53,520 90,920
Psychology Teachers, Postsecondary.	24,000	27,230	51,640 89,770
Sociology Teachers, Postsecondary.	13,760	25,780	48,010 81,780
History Teachers, Postsecondary.	16,630	28,180	49,080 83,730
Commercial and Industrial Designers.	33,910	27,290	48,780 77,790

Nuclear Medicine Technologists.	18,030	31,910	44,130	58,500
Anthropologists.	**4,140**	**21,880**	**36,040**	**62,430**
Computer Programmers.	530,730	35,020	57,590	93,210
Mathematical Technicians.	1,540	22,790	34,800	80,060
Management Analysts.	357,610	32,860	55,040	98,210
Environmental Scientists and Specialists, Including Health.	**54,860**	**28,520**	**44,180**	**73,790**
Electrical Engineers	162,400	41,740	64,910	94,490
Mining and Geological Engineers, Including Mining Safety Engineers.	6,690	36,070	60,820	100,050
Epidemiologists.	**2,480**	**31,070**	**48,390**	**78,630**
Medical Scientists, Except Epidemiologists.	**35,570**	**31,440**	**57,810**	**112,000**
Microbiologists.	15,880	30,420	48,890	84,790
Foresters.	9,890	27,330	43,640	65,960
English Language and Literature Teachers, Postsecondary.	50,560	24,000	44,310	78,390

Foreign Language and Literature Teachers, Postsecondary.	18,380	25,680	44,380 77,660
Biological Science Teachers, Postsecondary.	36,910	29,770	54,450 109,660
Forestry and Conservation Science Teachers, Postsecondary.	1,980	36,360	58,110 92,790
Industrial Engineers.	171,810	38,140	58,580 86,370
Archivists.			*(no data available)*
Veterinarians.	**40,270**	**36,670**	**60,910 128,720**
Biologists.			*(no data available)*
Hydrologists.	7,240	35,910	55,410 85,260
Geologists.	21,810	33,910	56,230 106,040
Health Specialties Teachers, Postsecondary.	78,680	29,550	59,220 130,190
Mathematicians.	**3,140**	**35,390**	**68,640 101,900**
Chemists.	**82,320**	**29,620**	**50,080 88,030**
Materials Scientists.	**8,660**	**33,120**	**60,620 99,820**
Educational Psychologists.	103,120	28,090	48,320 76,840

Judges, Magistrate Judges, and Magistrates.	25,190	19,320	86,760 134,660
Technical Writers.	50,700	28,890	47,790 74,360
Financial Analysts.	159,490	31,880	52,420 101,760
Plant Scientists.			*(no data available)*
Astronomers.	910	38,310	74,510 112,550
Engineering Teachers, Postsecondary.	26,940	35,540	65,640 107,980
Mathematical Science Teachers, Postsecondary.	37,660	25,290	47,440 85,010
Marine Architects.	4,680	35,640	60,890 89,760
Psychiatrists.	21,280	50,930	118,640 *
Chemistry Teachers, Postsecondary.	16,020	30,870	52,530 89,390
Computer Systems Analysts.	463,300	37,460	59,330 89,040
Aerospace Engineers.	71,550	47,700	67,930 94,310
Lawyers.	489,530	44,590	88,280 *
Statisticians.	17,520	28,430	51,990 86,660
Chemical Engineers.	31,530	45,200	65,960 93,430
Physics Teachers, Postsecondary.	11,880	32,640	58,500 103,290

Computer Science Teachers, Postsecondary.	27,770	24,980	46,890	85,490
Agricultural Engineers.	2,170	33,660	55,850	91,600
Nuclear Engineers.	12,610	58,030	79,360	105,930
Physicists.	**8,990**	**51,680**	**83,310**	**116,290**
Urban and Regional Planners.	**28,850**	**29,890**	**46,500**	**72,090**
Architects, Except Landscape and Naval.	74,390	32,540	52,510	85,670

*Indicates a salary greater than $145,000 per year.

Bold indicates this is a top job, based on both fit and/or total employment.

The jobs listed here are just the beginning. It is important to read through all the jobs for your temperament, and to browse the jobs for the other temperaments. This will ensure that you have identified your temperament correctly. Then, refer to chapter 12 for where to go from here.

WORKING THROUGH IT ALL

NOW YOU KNOW about temperament. Having identified your temperament and the role you primarily play at work, and knowing which jobs fit you best, you can begin the real work of finding or changing to a rewarding and satisfying career. Or, if you are already in a career you enjoy, you can begin to put together your knowledge of temperament and the people around you to create a better, more productive, and harmonious work environment.

PROCEEDING WITH YOUR JOB SEARCH

The list or lists that apply to you are only the beginning. Perhaps you have identified the perfect job title for you, with a salary range and skill level that fits your needs. Now what? The first place you should go is online to O*Net (see the resources section for a link) and search for that job title. From there, you can explore the activities, interests, skills, and values of the job in detail, to verify that it is the job you think it is. You can and should also explore "related jobs" to see if there is something even more appealing.

Then, if you are in school or otherwise looking for your very first job, you will want to visit your career development office to see what material and background information they have on that position in your area. There you will learn more specific regional salaries, working conditions, expected outlook for that career path, and local groups or organizations for that job. Talking to a counselor can help you focus and align the factors that are important to you with those required by employers.

Finding trade groups and talking to people already in the positions you are considering are your best resources, both for those new on the job market and those looking for a new career. If you don't know anyone who is currently in the job that appeals to you, you will want to find someone who is doing the work and can tell you what it is like. Ideally, you will want to find someone who shares the same values and interests that you do – someone of your temperament. If you do know someone, or several people, you will want to find out all you can from talking to them to confirm that occupation is right for you.

Another valuable resource is trade or professional publications. Usually these are put out by the job or industry group, and so will be current on the latest issues affecting workers in the job. If you have been interested in the position for a while, you may already be receiving trade, professional, or enthusiast publications that relate to the job. These resources will also let you know the levels of skill and training for these jobs successful people have, and can point you toward any trainings, certifications, or education you will need.

Putting It Together At Work

Being successful in our jobs, careers, or life vocations will depend a great deal on how well we know ourselves. Knowing our personality allows us to align the interests, skills, and values we hold with the work that we do. Each temperament and every individual displays different strengths and weaknesses. In working together, it is much better to focus on the strengths we have and put those to good use, rather than identifying weakness and trying to mold people to jobs for which they are not suited. You cannot change people – at least not for long and not in a way that will ultimately benefit the organization or endeavor.

Each work setting or project is a dynamic system, with interdependencies based on the structure and circumstances of the tasks, resources, and people. There is no linear prediction for how to assemble the "perfect" team to accomplish a goal, because the nature of the tasks and the results you get will change based on the team you put together. The best we can do is to assemble a team which works well together, which has the skills required to accomplish the tasks, which is made up of people who hold interests and values complementary to the project, and then give guidance and feedback along the way. The results of this approach may not always be what we expect, but they may often surprise you and surpass your initial projections. Dynamic systems, like our society composed of different personalities, have a way of taking on a life of their own.

The four temperaments are interrelated, as we are all human and share greater than 99% of our DNA with each other. It is the subtle and not-so-subtle observations of behavior that point the way to the similarities and differences among and between us. Each temperament can be thought of in terms of two of the other temperaments (and the opposite of the third):

> Artisan – utilitarian Guardian; concrete Rational
> (not Idealist).
> Guardian – cooperative Artisan; concrete Idealist
> (not Rational).
> Rational – abstract Artisan; utilitarian Idealist
> (not Guardian).
> Idealist – abstract Guardian; cooperative Rational
> (not Artisan).

If you know a person of one temperament, say an Artisan, and how they function in a particular role, then knowing another person is a Guardian would provide you with a clue as to how they might function in that same role, namely in a less utilitarian, more cooperative way, but both will be concrete.

Dynamic systems exist in time, and each of the temperaments has a unique orientation toward time. We see the Guardian time roles played out at work: maintaining the procedures and regulations and applying judgment based on concrete expectations developed in the past. Artisans are always looking for future opportunity and advantage in any direction. They are not linearly directed and do not regard the past as a guide. Rationals, with their focus on elemental facts of science, look forward in a way that does not rely on the past, but on "timeless" principles. The Idealist is difficult to pin down, pulling their orientation from the past, the future, and the present. Their relationship to time is based on bringing all three dimensions into a whole, in a non-linear way.

And so, we have the innate characteristics of each of the temperaments' relationship to time: The Guardian is linear in looking to the past as a guide for the present and future. The Artisan is now, without direction, in looking toward the future. The Rational is eternal, directed toward the timeless, in looking toward the future. The Idealist is all of these things – and none of them – looking not toward any direction but in all of them, focused not on the past or the future, but both – simultaneously – in the present. The Guardian is traditionalistic, the Artisan opportunistic, the Rational futuristic, and the Idealist holistic.

There are no strict criteria for managing or working with people of different temperaments. Trial and error, on a temperament and individual basis, is still going to serve you best. But knowing the temperaments of those you work with, and that how they behave is part of their makeup, just like the color of their eyes, can help you keep a perspective and resist the temptation to change your coworkers into a copy of yourself or an ideal of someone else.

✼ ✼ ✼

Keeping the innate, unchangeable, and special traits you have foremost in mind as you proceed through your life and career will serve you well. This is not new advice, but I hope that some of the knowledge and tools presented here will be a strong first step. There are many practical considerations and compromises we must make every day, but if we take time to stop and evaluate what is really important, we can stay on path – whichever path is ours. Shakespeare said it best,

"This above all: To thine own self be true."

RESOURCES

<u>PERSONALITY</u>

When I first discovered my personality type 20 years ago, there were few resources for individuals. Now, there are many web sites and books dedicated to various typing theories, containing everything from pop quizzes to valid assessments. I list a few of the best here, but please note that web sites are very fluid, and anything printed here may be different or not exist by the time you read this.

- Keirsey, David. *Please Understand Me II*. Del Mar, CA: Prometheus Nemesis, 1998.
- Keirsey, David and Bates, Marilyn. *Please Understand Me: Character & Temperament Types* (Fifth Edition). Del Mar, CA: Prometheus Nemesis, 1978.

Both of the above can be ordered from Matrix Books, Inc. at http://www.matrixbooksinc.com.

To discover your type, the Keirsey Temperament Sorter™ II is available through AdvisorTeam.com, Inc. You can take the Sorter for free to discover your temperament, or pay a fee for a full type report. Web site: **http://www.advisorteam.com.**

More type and temperament information is also available at the web site of Dr. Keirsey's son, Dr. David Keirsey, Jr. at **http://www.keirsey.com.**

It Takes All Types

To learn your Myers Briggs personality type, you can visit your high school or college counseling office, and they can usually refer you to a certified administrator. You can also take the Myers Briggs Type Indicator® online in several places, one being the web site at **http://www.knowyourtype.com.**

Career

One of the best resources available to you is your local community college or library. If you are in school, then your high school or college career counseling center should be first on your list. If you can't get to one of those places, or just want more information, you can start with either of these books, both of which are excellent resources in their own right:

- Lore, Nicholas. *The Pathfinder: how to choose or change your career for a lifetime of satisfaction and success.* New York, NY: Fireside, 1998.
- Bolles, Richard N. *What Color Is Your Parachute?: a practical manual for job hunters and career changers.* Berkeley, CA: Ten Speed Press, 2003.

Finally, for professionals and power users, there is the o*net™ Resource Center available online at the web site **http://www.onetcenter.org.**

BIBLIOGRAPHY

Gandhi, Modandas (Mahadev Desai, translator). *An Autobiography: The Story of My Experiments with Truth*. Boston, MA: Beacon Press, 1993.

Gardner, Howard. *Frames of Mind: The Theory of Multiple Intelligences*. New York, NY: Basic Books, 1993.

Gerhy, Frank, quoted in Robert Ivy, "Interview: Frank Gehry," *Architectural Record* May, 1999.

Isachsen, Olaf. *Joining the Entrepreneurial Elite: Four Styles to Business Success*. Palo Alto, CA: Consulting Psychologists Press, 1996.

Keirsey, David. *Please Understand Me II*. Del Mar, CA: Prometheus Nemesis, 1998.

Keirsey, David and Bates, Marilyn. *Please Understand Me: Character & Temperament Types* (Fifth Edition). Del Mar, CA: Prometheus Nemesis, 1978.

Patton, George. *War As I Knew It*. New York, NY: Mariner Books, 1995.

Plomin, R., DeDFries, J., McClearn, G. and McGuffin, P. *Behavioral Genetics* (Fourth Edition). New York, NY: Worth Publishers, 2001.

ABOUT THE AUTHOR

JOHN ARNOPP is a strategic marketing and financial analyst for a large financial services company. Previously, he held the position of vice president of business strategy & development for an online personality consulting company and distributor of the Keirsey Temperament Sorter.

John spent the first part of his career in public health, working for a state-run genetic screening program. While there, he co-authored several scientific papers. Subsequently, John worked as a financial analyst and wrote several articles on various investment topics. John has also held management positions at an Internet software company he co-founded and an online medical information company, where he served in both business development and marketing roles.

John has studied and written about personality theory and Dr. Keirsey's work for 20 years. He holds a Bachelor of Science degree in Genetics from the University of California, Berkeley. John is also a lifelong Rational.

Printed in the United States
1535500004B/313-315